D0474658

Access All Areas:
disability, technology and learning

Edited by Lawrie Phipps, Allan Sutherland and Jane Seale

Acknowledgements

The publication of this book is the result of a collaboration between TechDis and the Association for Learning Technology who have worked together to commission and edit the contributions. Both TechDis and the Association for Learning Technology would like to acknowledge the following people who have contributed chapters for this book:

David Banes	AbilityNet
Simon Ball	TechDis
Nigel Beacham	IMPACT Research Group, Loughborough University
Chris Cann	Educational Consultant
Margaret Dilloway	Bournville College of Further Education
EA Draffan	TechDis Accessibility Database
Shirley Evans	Royal National College for the Blind
Philip Henderson	ICT Access Specialist, Treloar Trust
Michael Lakey	Tynemouth College
AP McDermott	Communications and Learning Technologies Research Group, University of Plymouth
Zoë Neumann	Royal National Institute for the Blind
Susi Peacock	Learning Technology Advisor, Queen Margaret University College
Daniel Ross	WebCT Administrator, Queen Margaret University College
Jacqui Skelton	Student Disability Advisor, Queen Margaret University College
David Sloan	Digital Media Access Group
Stuart Smith	MIMAS, Manchester Computing, University of Manchester
Mike Wald	Director Southern Higher and Further Education Collaboration
Betty Willder	JISC Legal Information Service
Kathy Wiles	LTSN Generic Centre
NAJ Witt	Communications and Learning Technologies Research Group, University of Plymouth

The following contributed to the reviewing, copy editing or proof reading of this book and their comments and assistance are also gratefully acknowledged:

Simon Ball	TechDis
Samuel Fanous	Oxford University
Rhonda Rhiachi	Director, Association for Learning Technology

Design and DTP by jamietshaw@hotmail.com

A note on language

There are many terms in current usage to describe disabled people. In this publication we have used the term 'impairment' to cover the range of conditions which lead to a person being disabled. An impairment is therefore some part of a person's physical being or learning ability, which does not function in the same way as most people's. This can include a wide range of visual impairments, hearing impairments (covering both deaf and hard of hearing), mobility impairments, medical conditions (for example epilepsy or asthma) and cognitive or learning issues (for example dyslexia).

However, the language regarding disabilities must be carefully chosen. We have used the term 'disabled people' (or students) rather than, for example, 'people with disabilities', as it very much changes the emphasis of ownership or cause of the disability. The term 'people with disabilities' implies that the person's impairment or condition causes them to be 'disabled' (and consequently that it is their responsibility to overcome it), whereas 'disabled person' implies that the person is disabled not necessarily by their condition or impairment, but by society and its inability or reluctance to cater effectively for that person (and consequently that society must effect change to remove that disability).

Following this logically it is acceptable to refer to a 'person with an impairment' because the ownership lies with the person (a deaf person is unable to hear, that is their impairment, whereas the fact that they experience barriers to functioning normally within society is a societal problem and hence they become disabled by those barriers, not by their impairment directly).

The differences between the terms may seem subtle to some people, but to disabled people they are extremely important. Different people and organisations choose different language and most have rational arguments to defend their choice. Hopefully the explanation given here shows why we have chosen the terminology that you will find within this publication.

Foreword

This publication provides a useful and timely resource for the post-16 education sector, with the arrival of the Special Educational Needs and Disability Act. It draws on the experiences of practitioners from a wide range of colleges, universities and JISC services to provide pragmatic advice on how to support disabled students when accessing technology and, perhaps more importantly, when accessing learning through technology.

I would like to thank the wide range of specialists that have contributed to this publication. TechDis has brought together staff who directly support disabled students, staff who use technology to support learning and staff involved in research to provide viewpoints across the spectrum of institutional activities. It is important that this dialogue continues and that all staff develop strategies for working together to support disabled learners.

Finally it should be remarked that many of the practices contained in this publication have much wider implications than meeting the requirements of legislation. Embedding the principles of good practice illustrated within this publication will be of benefit not only to disabled students but also to all students, ensuring universal access to all areas of learning.

Dr Malcolm Read
Joint Information Systems Committee

Within the student groups that we work with or support it is increasingly likely that some will have a disability. The changing climate within further and higher education is such that meeting the needs of disabled students can no longer be seen as an optional extra that some of us provide if we have some personal experience of the disability in question or are feeling 'charitable'. Changes in legislation mean that meeting the needs of disabled students should now be a core activity of all further and higher education providers.

This book is designed to outline and describe how technologies can be used to meet the needs of disabled students. It will focus on two important issues. Firstly, how assistive technology can facilitate access to learning resources and teaching material. Secondly, how e-learning materials and learning technologies that utilise the Web need to be carefully designed so that all students can benefit from using them. The book will provide an overview of these technologies, how they can be used by disabled students and also how their design could be improved to benefit all students, not just those with a disability. This overview will be placed within the context of UK and European legislation and will also include some illustrative case studies.

Whilst the book concentrates on technological issues, these issues cannot be seen in isolation from the broader context of changing the attitudes and practice of those who work with or support disabled students. Hall and Tinklin (1998) presented some case studies of the experiences of disabled students in Scottish Higher Education. One of those case studies involved a student called Sandy who has a hearing impairment. She described how she struggled to get a lecturer to wear a radio microphone and was really embarrassed at having to explain herself to the lecturer in front of the other students:

"With 150 people you're sitting there and I'm sure my face went red. I didn't look around, I thought if I look around everybody's going to be sitting looking at me. I could just have run out of the room, but then I would have gained nothing by that. It just made me angry and hurt… I thought God, have I got to do this in every one of these lectures?… one day he'll wear it the next day he won't wear it." (Hall and Tinklin 1998)

If the lecturer referred to in this quote should read this book we would hope that they (along with other lecturers, learning technologists, librarians etc.) would gain an understanding of the legal imperatives for changing their practice (for instance why a radio microphone is so important for students like Sandy), as well as other ways in which they might make teaching and learning material more accessible for all the students that they teach.

Lawrie Phipps, TechDis
Allan Sutherland, TechDis
Jane Seale, University of Southampton and Kings College, London

July 2002

Hall, J. and Tinklin, T. (1998), Students First: The Experiences of Disabled Students in Higher Education. SCRE Research Report No 85, available from:
www.scre.ac.uk/resreport/rr85/index.html

Contents

Section 5: Implications for personal and professional practice

Accessibility and inclusivity in further and higher education: an overview

Chapter 1

David Banes, AbilityNet
Jane Seale, University of Southampton and Kings College, London

1.1 Introduction

Most official documents and reports covering the educational needs of disabled students mention the terms accessibility and inclusivity. As with many well-used terms in further and higher education these are jargon or buzz-words that many people use but few understand in depth. This chapter will seek to provide a context for these two terms. It will outline the political, theoretical and practical background to these terms and in doing so will provide an introduction for the remaining chapters of the book.

1.2 Widening participation and disability legislation

The Disability Discrimination Act (1995) (DDA) was passed in the UK to introduce new legislation aimed at ending the discrimination that many disabled people face [1]. The main focus of the Act was the employment of disabled people and their access to goods and services. However, the Act did affect further and higher education institutions to the extent that in their capacity as 'service providers' they had to make 'reasonable adjustments' to the way they provided their services to make them accessible to disabled people. In 1997, the Dearing Report reflected the spirit of the DDA when it argued that access to education should be widened in order to include students who might previously have been disadvantaged because of their socio-economic status, gender, ability level, ethnic background, geographic location or special educational needs [2]. Both the DDA and the Dearing Report served

to contribute to a climate in which some further and higher education institutions began to think about how they could make their learning environments more accessible and in doing so 'include' more disabled students. For example, Davies [3] described some of the activities undertaken by the University of North London in order to provide inclusive and accessible education for all its students. This included working with an access consultant when constructing a new 'Technology Tower'. The 'Tower' was designed to provide physical access for disabled people and be comfortable and easy for them to use:

"…the ideal was to provide an inclusive working environment where disabled students could work with their peers rather than being segregated into special areas. This goal has been substantially achieved although there are some specialist workstations for those who require height adjustable tables and access to specialist software. We are now in the process of ensuring that the operating systems within the Tower are user-friendly for disabled students – this will include security cards, emergency evacuation and booking systems as well as technical support."

The Special Educational Needs and Disability Act (2001) (SENDA) amended the 1995 DDA to include education. The teaching and learning components come into force in September 2002. SENDA will have a major impact upon education provision within further and higher education, and will require them to address in more detail the accessibility of their learning resources and teaching materials. In Chapter 2, Willder will address in more detail the legal implications of this new Act, and in Chapter 3, Ball will place the Act within the context of recent European Union policy and initiatives.

1.3 Facilitating access through the use of assistive technology

One of the ways in which access to learning resources and teaching material can be facilitated is through the use of specialised technologies often called assistive technology. Assistive technology can be defined as:

> "equipment and software that are used to maintain or improve the functional capabilities of a person with a disability" [4]

In thinking about how assistive technology can facilitate access to learning resources or teaching material, the focus is on providing access to technologies that will bridge the 'access gap' between the teaching material and the student. The material itself may not have to be altered if appropriate assistive technologies can be utilised.

For students in further and higher education the kinds of assistive technology they may need to use include:

 ▶ technology that facilitates access to a standard PC,
 ▶ technology that facilitates access to the Internet,
 ▶ technology that facilitates access to and manipulation of written word,
 ▶ technology that facilitates access to and manipulation of spoken word,
 ▶ technology that helps to compensate for cognitive deficits.

Assistive technology includes hardware such as scanners, adapted keyboards or hearing aids and software such as speech recognition software or thought organisation software. Assistive technology is often associated with high-tech systems such as speech recognition software, but it can include low-tech solutions such as arm wrests or wrist guards.

1.3.1 Facilitating access to a standard PC
Most subjects include some element of IT use within the curriculum and any student who cannot

access that technology will immediately be at a disadvantage. Obvious examples include image manipulation in the graphic arts, composition in music and satellite data in travel and tourism. In addition, most further and higher education institutions expect their students to present their coursework and assignments in printed form. It is unusual nowadays to encounter a student who is not recording, reporting, retrieving or communicating their work using a PC. Not all students can afford their own equipment and many will use their institution's own, often restricted, resources.

Computer use can appear to be unachievable for some disabled people. However, the problem usually lies with the design or implementation of the interface to the computer. A standard computer laboratory or workshop might contain banks of identical computers, each with a standard keyboard, mouse, monitor and desktop. However, the size, needs and abilities of each user are not standardised. Fortunately, a modern computer is an immensely flexible tool, and there are a wide range of adaptations that can be used to tailor the computer to the user. It is essential that support departments are aware of what is available and what is possible – a computer should be adapted to the needs of the user, not the other way round.

For individuals with a physical, cognitive, learning, hearing or visual disability (for example, Repetitive Strain Injury, dyslexia or colour-blindness) the standard screen, keyboard, mouse and/or desktop may be uncomfortable, unproductive or even impossible to access. The user may find that simply being left-handed means the standard kit is awkward to use. Solutions to access problems may range from a simple guard to stop more than one key being pressed at the same time, to a different shape or size of keyboard. There are mouse alternatives such as joysticks and tracker balls, voice recognition software, keyboard emulation, on-screen keyboards with switch input, and screen reading systems, many of which are now relatively inexpensive and reliable.

Before considering purchasing assistive technology, however, it is worth looking much more closely at the accessibility features built into operating systems such as Microsoft Windows. A standard keyboard is designed to be used with two hands, it favours right-handed people (as the numeric keyboard is located on the right) and can be 'over sensitive', producing a string of letters instead of the intended one character if the key is held down for too long. The Microsoft Windows operating system offers free solutions to these and other problems. For example, many software programs require the user to press two or three keys down simultaneously, an impossible task for the one-fingered or mouthstick user. The 'Sticky Keys' option within Windows allows the user to press one key at a time and instructs Windows to respond as if the keys had been pressed in combination. Other features such as 'Slow Keys', 'Bounce Keys' and 'Repeat Keys' adjust the sensitivity of the keyboard in ways that can help those individuals with dexterity problems such as slow reaction times or tremors [5]. In Chapter 7, Henderson will discuss in more detail alternatives to mouse and keyboard input that can benefit physically disabled students.

1.3.2 Examples of assistive technology in use

Christopher has a visual impairment and finds standard computer kit onerous to use. He benefits from a larger monitor and some of the Windows high visibility background and text colour schemes, adjusting contrast and font size as appropriate. With the addition of text magnification and screen reading technology, as well as an OCR (optical character recognition) scanner with a facility for speaking written text, Christopher is producing the quality of work of which he is capable. In Chapter 4, Neumann provides a more in depth overview of the types of assistive technology that visually impaired students might benefit from using.

Emily is a student who has ME (chronic fatigue syndrome) and struggles with tiredness and the associated lack of concentration. Although computers are available in her institution, demand outstrips supply and Emily finds it difficult to work 'to order', especially when there are people around waiting to use the equipment. Emily has used her DSA (Disabled Students Allowance) to buy her own PC, which she accesses with a small keyboard. Typing and proof reading work is minimised through the use of software modifications including an auto-correction facility and templates. In addition, Emily can use a speech recognition package for 'hands free' computing. Finally, 'Texthelp, Read and Write' has been installed on her machine. This has a number of useful functions including word prediction and homophone checking, and will speak text audibly for proofing. In Chapter 5, Wald illustrates how speech recognition systems and other technologies can assist students with a hearing impairment.

Keira is both dyslexic and dyspraxic, conditions that affect her ability to record information accurately and to control a mouse and keyboard

effectively. She is now using an adaptive solution that meets her needs. This includes a small keyboard and trackerball, which she finds much easier to operate than a standard keyboard and mouse. A scanner with OCR and 'Texthelp Read and Write' enable her to listen to her work and hear text documents rather than having to read them. She also uses a 'brainstorming' package that allows her to enter her ideas and convert them into an action list – a major advantage for a student with a disability that impairs her ability to plan efficiently. Keira finds the auto-correction facility and templates useful features that can speed up the writing process by avoiding re-entering often-used blocks of text and phrases.

Another example of equipment which students find useful is a reader pen – a light, hand-held version of a scanner which, when linked to other software, can provide an immediate spoken definition of a new word. In Chapter 6, Draffan provides a more in-depth overview of the types of assistive technology that dyslexic students might benefit from using. In Chapter 10, Smith discusses issues that arise from dyslexic students using Virtual Learning Environments, and in Chapter 16 Beacham illustrates how the design of computer based learning materials for dyslexic students can be theory driven.

1.4 Facilitating inclusivity through Universal Design

Assistive technologies are specialised pieces of equipment or software designed specifically for disabled users. There is a growing recognition, however, that if general everyday products and environments were designed differently so that the majority of people could use them, there would be less need for this specialised equipment. This principle is called Universal Design or Design-for-All and is strongly linked to the concept of inclusivity. Universal Design can be defined as:

"The design of products and environments that can be used and experienced by people of all ages and abilities, to the greatest extent possible, without adaptation"

Products designed using the principles of Universal Design:

▶ are developed with consideration of the needs of a diverse population,
▶ are not described as being anything more than easy for everyone to use,

- are always accessible (but because accessibility has been integrated from the beginning of the design process, they are less likely to be noticeable),
- benefit everyone, not only disabled people.

Brenda Smith and Alan Hurst in the book "Accessible Curricula: Good Practice for All" have a vision for the future that strongly echoes the underlying principles of Universal Design:

> "We are moving slowly but steadily to the position where it will be fair to claim that we have fully inclusive high quality policy and provisions for students with disabilities and/or learning difficulties in higher education. Access for all has become access to excellence for all." [4]

In thinking about how Universal Design can facilitate inclusivity, the focus is on whether and how learning resources and teaching material can be designed or organized differently. For students in tertiary education principles of Universal Design have the potential to impact upon:

- **Design and delivery of teaching material delivered via the Web.** In Chapter 8 Sloan provides an overview of several tools and techniques for providing accessible Web-based e-learning materials, while in Chapter 9 Witt and McDermott provide a detailed account of how to approach making Web sites compliant with the new anti-discrimination legislation. In Chapter 17 Lakey provides an example of an institutional Web policy that attempts to address the requirements for accessibility and inclusivity.
- **Design and delivery of Virtual Learning Environments.** In Chapter 10, Smith discusses the accessibility of VLEs with specific reference to dyslexic students, while in Chapter 11 Cann, Ball and Sutherland present the results of a TechDis survey which attempted to ascertain how accessible a number commercially available VLEs are.
- **Design and delivery of computer assisted assessments.** In Chapter 13 Wiles looks at the accessibility issues raised by the increased use of automated and online assessment.

1.4.1 Universal Web site design

The design principles behind accessible Web sites do not only benefit people with disabilities. Those with eyestrain or tiredness, the elderly or those with a slow Internet connection can all benefit from their application. For those responsible for designing Web-based educational material it is essential that they attempt to integrate greater flexibility, including a wide range of access methods, to allow the individual to choose the most appropriate solution for their needs and abilities. In many cases, designers are starting work without a clear understanding of Universal Design and accessibility issues.

AbilityNet has recently undertaken an extensive review of over 30 Web sites finding examples of both good and poor practice. Sites that were found to be accessible exhibited an uncluttered page layout and appropriate colour contrasts. User-friendly sites also used 'Access Keys', which enable keyboard users to quickly select the link they require without having to 'tab' repeatedly, as well as providing pages explaining how to change browser settings to increase text size and change colours for ease of viewing and interpretation. In some cases a 'text only' version of the site's contents was offered – a bonus to those using screen reading technology, particularly if the graphics were present only for decoration.

Many sites were inaccessible for a range of reasons. Some failed to attach an 'alt tag' to each graphic – essential for those not viewing images, using a text-based browser or a screen reader. An 'alt tag' automatically pops up to describe the image when the mouse passes over it – particularly useful when the graphic is a link to other pages.

It is important to acknowledge that increasing accessibility does not mean compromising the impact and creativity of design, it is a matter of awareness and sensitivity to the issues involved. AbilityNet's experience would suggest that once designers are aware of the issues, the technologies used and the solutions on offer, they feel able to implement accessibility measures rapidly, effectively and imaginatively [6]. In Chapter 12 Peacock, Ross and Skelton describe how they have used a Virtual Learning Environment to create a staff development module aimed at increasing academic staff's awareness of accessibility legislation and its implication for creating online teaching and learning materials. In Chapters 14 and 15 the authors examine the experience of e-tutoring disabled students.

1.5 Conclusions

This chapter has provided a broad framework within which to apply and interpret the terms accessibility and inclusivity. The remaining chapters will expand on many of the issues we have raised in order to provide a more detailed picture of how all those who work with and support disabled students can work towards creating more accessible and inclusive learning materials and environments.

1.6 References

[1]   Disability Discrimination Act (1995), available from:
      **www.hmso.gov.uk/acts/acts1995/
      1995050.htm**

[2]   Dearing, R. (1997), Higher Education in the Learning Society: Report of the National Committee of Inquiry into Higher Education, Sheffield, DfEE.

[3]   Davies, C. (2000), Making learning technologies accessible to disabled students, ALT-N 28, p3.

[4]   Doyle, C. and Robson, K. (2002), Accessible Curricula: Good Practice for All, Cardiff, University of Wales Institute, available from:
      www.techdis.ac.uk/pdf/curricula.pdf

[5]   AbilityNet Skill Sheet, Accessibility in Windows, available from:
      **www.abilitynet.co.uk/content/
      factsheets/Factsheets.htm**

[6]   AbilityNet Fact Sheet, Accessible Web Design, available from:
      **www.abilitynet.co.uk/content/
      factsheets/Factsheets.htm**

2

Setting the context: legislation, policy and standards

Chapter 2

Disability legislation: implications for learning technologists in the UK

Betty Willder, JISC Legal Information Service

2.1 Introduction

The implementation of the Disability Discrimination Act (1995) has meant that further and higher education institutions have already been involved to an extent in addressing the legal implications of disability discrimination. For example, employees in the sector have been covered by Part 2 of the Act. Also, where the institution provides services other than education, Part 3 of the Act is also in force. The principles of the Special Educational Needs and Disability Act (2001), which comes into force in September 2002 are therefore not new. What is new is that the principles of the new Act directly apply to the provision of education services, which includes traditional activities such as lectures and also e-learning.

This chapter addresses the legal implications of the new Act and seeks to provide an overview of the effects of Act on the education sector at both an institutional level and a personal level. The Act and the responsibilities under it affect the whole spectrum of those involved in the sector – those providing the information, those providing the media for the information and those involved in IT services and strategy all have equal responsibility under the legislation. The legislation affects the provision of Information Technology and Computing Services in the very widest sense of the phrase and ignoring the legislation is not an option.

2.2 What does the legislation say?

The Special Educational Needs and Disability Act (2001) amends the Disability Discrimination Act

(1995) and will be implemented as Part 4 of that Act. Parts 1, 2 and 3 are already in force. Briefly, from September 1st 2002, the Act makes it an offence to discriminate against a disabled person by treating him or her less favourably than others for a reason relating to their disability. For the purposes of the legislation a disabled person is defined as someone who has a physical or mental impairment, which has an effect on his or her ability to carry out normal day-to-day activities.

The Act covers all aspects of an institution's student services. 'Student services' is given a broad meaning of 'services of any description which are provided wholly or mainly for students' and will obviously include educational services such as teaching and learning provision. What constitutes an institution is defined broadly in the Act but is likely to include most further and higher education institutions providing post-16 education in the UK with the exception of Northern Ireland.

2.3 What is discrimination?

In this legislation, discrimination is described as occurring where, for a reason related to his or her disability, a person is treated 'less favourably' than someone without that disability and such treatment cannot be justified. Discrimination can also occur where an institution fails to make a 'reasonable adjustment' where the disabled student is placed at a 'substantial disadvantage' in comparison with someone who is not disabled and such failure cannot be 'justified'.

Discrimination or 'less favourable' treatment does

not occur if the institution does not know or could not have been reasonably expected to know that the student was disabled. However, legal opinion differs on when an institution can be deemed to know (for example if a student told a cleaner) and there are also confidentiality issues to be considered.

As has already been well documented elsewhere, it is also too soon to be able to interpret the meanings of the terms 'less favourable', 'substantially disadvantaged' and 'justified'. Although substantive case law is necessary to provide guidance on the interpretation of the terms in the Act, if the experience of the Australian system (which is approximately five years ahead of the UK) is anything to go by, cases will fortunately be few. The institutions there appear to be working reasonably satisfactorily within the law, which is ideally the position the UK institutions should aim to achieve. However, cases have been brought and these may be used in support of any UK legal action. While case law would clarify the situation it would also be undesirable for any particular institution to become embroiled in such a situation.

2.4 What is a 'reasonable adjustment'?

2.4.1 Web sites
The World Wide Web Consortium (W3C) has a Web Accessibility Initiative outlining different levels of accessibility. Commentators have suggested that Priority 1 and Priority 2 of their guidelines should be the norm and it may be expedient for institutions to be anticipating the likelihood that the courts may use this as a standard when deciding what is a 'reasonable adjustment'.

However, as many learning technologists will be aware, many electronic resources used in learning and teaching are not held by the host institution. Linking from the institution's 'compliant' e-learning material to an external source that is non-compliant may present difficulties. Questions may need to be considered as to whether the material is core course material and if so it may be discriminatory action by the University not to provide it in an alternative format.

There is some evidence from the US that the unfortunate solution, adopted there by some colleges to avoid potential liability, is to remove the link. Whilst there is no clear answer to this, as

the legislation matures more guidance will become available.

2.4.2 Use of assistive technology
Technologies are available to assist users with special needs and it is up to each institution to anticipate the need and to provide assistance. An institution must make 'reasonable adjustments' and hence use of assistive technology will become the norm. If a legal action is raised alleging discrimination, it is likely that a court may look to the practice in other institutions and to relevant codes of practice and industry standards in coming to a decision as to what may be considered 'reasonable adjustments'.

A wheelchair user may reasonably request that an adjustable desk be provided to enable access to a PC and extra hardware may also be requested. It is likely that this would be considered a 'reasonable' request that should be granted. It may also be considered good practice and expedient for an institution to be aware of the financial help which may be available to assist individual students and therefore be beneficial in allowing the institution to restrict its financial outlay. For example, the Disabled Students Allowance may be applicable to some students. However it would be an unwise institution which relied totally on these allowances as they are only of limited applicability and do not override an institution's legal requirement to anticipate and make 'reasonable adjustments' for disabled students.

2.5 What is the anticipatory element to the Act?

The anticipatory element of the Act places the onus on an institution to anticipate and pre-empt the needs of the potential student even though the institutions may consider that it has no disabled students at present. For example an institution should try to ensure that Web sites and course materials are accessible and can be delivered in alternative formats if requested in the future.

2.6 When is less favourable treatment justifiable?

As with the majority of legislation there are exceptions. The responsibility to make a 'reasonable adjustment' under SENDA (2001) may be diluted or avoided in certain circum-stances. Less favourable treatment even after making 'reasonable adjustments' may not be regarded as discriminatory in the following situations:

▶ if the less favourable treatment is necessary to maintain academic standards or other prescribed standards,
▶ if the cost of the adjustment is prohibitive with regard to availability of financial resources,
▶ if the adjustment affects the interests of other students,
▶ if the adjustment impacts upon health and safety.

With time, there will be more substantive indicators of acceptable practice. However, it is very unlikely that any of the above will prove to be an easy way for institutions to opt-out of their responsibility under the Act, and should not be relied upon to provide a blanket means of avoiding new practices and provision.

2.7 What effect will the legislation have on Information Technology provision and use in the UK institutions?

Information Technology permeates every area of the modern educational establishment and the (non definitive) list below illustrates the way the legislation also permeates every aspect of educational services an institution:

▶ marketing,
▶ student Admissions and Registry Office,
▶ library and Information Services,
▶ academic departments and curriculum development,
▶ IT Services and strategy departments.

2.7.1 Marketing
Information for prospective students including learning through online provision should be user-friendly to the prospective student who may be disabled. An institution may possibly be considered as discriminating against disabled people if it does not anticipate the likelihood that a prospective student may have special needs and seek to address them.

2.7.2 Registry and admissions
A student application form needs to be user-friendly and ought to encourage disclosure of any disability, which may affect the student's educational experience. Confidential help should be available and ample opportunity and

encouragement in place for disclosure of a disability to an appropriate member of staff. The disabled student needs to be aware of, and realise the need for disclosure, in order to be provided with the best possible assistance.

2.7.3 Academic departments
Lecturers should be prepared to assist by providing lecture notes in alternative formats. Departmental policy and training may help in raising awareness. It may be worth ensuring that your departmental Web site is at least as user-friendly as that of the institution. Course materials should be available in alternative formats and provisions may need to be put in place for use of assistive technology in examination and assessment.

2.7.4 Library services
Increasingly library staff are involved in the teaching process and in provision of Web-based information. As such, the same accessibility issues arise as for academic departments.

2.7.5 IT services and strategy
Assistive hardware and software is available but can be costly. Financial strategy and general planning to anticipate the needs of the students is essential. Awareness of the numbers of students with special needs at your institution, anticipating future numbers and effecting changes to anticipate the needs of such students are all now essential elements in planning strategy.

2.8 Conclusions

The application and effect of the Special Educational Needs and Disability Act (2001) is in its infancy and brings new responsibilities for institutions. Planning, strategy and training may be seen as essential to cope with the effects of the legislation. Students will become more aware of their rights under the legislation and institutions must be prepared to handle this.

There is an anticipatory aspect to the legislation, which requires institutions to consider across the board adjustments to avoid future discrimination whilst still also meeting the needs of individual students.

It may be a defence against a charge of discrimination that an institution did not know that a student was disabled. This defence is unlikely to be successful if an institution did not take reasonable steps to find out and encourage disclosure in an atmosphere of confidentiality.

The legislation was introduced to ensure that disabled people have the same opportunities as non-disabled people and it is expected that the educational community should do as much as possible to ensure that this happens. Institutions should also be ascertaining now, how others are anticipating the needs of the students. If another institution facilitates the use of laptops in examinations is there a valid reason why your institution is unable to do so?

Training of staff and awareness-raising is vital in satisfactory implementation of the legislation and avoidance of liability for discrimination. As previously stated, the legal and academic sectors are currently trying to evaluate the meaning of the terms of the legislation, but no real interpretation will be available until the legislation matures or if there are test cases in the UK courts.

the attention of the sector to any substantive case law and other developments via the Web site as soon as available.

2.9 Resources

[1]   Disability Rights Commission: A draft Code of Practice (post 16) may be found here and gives working examples of what it regards as discriminatory and non-discriminatory practice. It is an easy to read guide and the final version is expected to be available shortly: **www.drc-gb.org/drc/default.asp**

[2]   JISC Legal Information Service: a JISC funded service providing information to the further and higher education sectors on the implications of the law on IT. The Service disseminates its information through its Web site and enquiry service and through workshops and other events and may be contacted at: legalinfo@ces.strath.ac.uk

[3]   JISC Senior Management Briefing Paper 15: Disability, Technology and Legislation: **www.jisc.ac.uk/pub01/smbp15.html**

[4]   TechDis: a JISC funded service, which seeks to improve access to further and higher education by the use of technology. Several articles covering specific areas of the legislation and technology can be found on the TechDis Web site **www.techdis.ac.uk**

[5]   The Special Educational Needs and Disability Act (2001): text is available from: **www.hmso.gov.uk/acts/acts2001/ 010010.htm**

The JISC Legal Information Service intends to publish an extended version of this chapter on its Web site at **www.jisc.ac.uk/legal/** and will draw

Chapter 3

The view from Europe: a TechDis perspective on how European initiatives will impact on education, technology and disabilities

Simon Ball, TechDis

3.1 Introduction

The European Union is becoming increasingly focussed on the dual agendas of widening participation in education and Design-for-All. In terms of increasing access to education for people with disabilities these two themes run in parallel to encourage Member States and the institutions within them to focus their attention on this area over the next few years. This chapter will outline the latest European initiatives and legislation that may have an impact on further and higher education institutions within the United Kingdom work towards increasing accessibility and inclusivity.

3.2 You can teach an old continent new tricks

The eEurope Action Plan for 2002 [1], agreed by Heads of State and Government, declares that "special attention should be given to disabled people and the fight against 'info-exclusion'" and that "public sector Web sites and their content in Member States… must be designed to be accessible to ensure that citizens with disabilities can access information…". A Ministerial Declaration from November 2001 [2] takes note of various reports on the topic of e-Inclusion and concurs that "greater account must be taken of specific needs, for example of the physically disabled". In the UK Education Sector this means that e-information must be accessible to all people with disabilities (not just students), for example a college or university Web site. In UK legislation it is likely that this will be enforced under parts 3 and 4 of the Disability Discrimination Act (1995).

3.3 Commitments

Member States of the European Union by definition have an obligation under Declaration 22 of the Amsterdam Treaty [3] to take into account the needs of disabled people. Measures are currently being implemented to apply this commitment in the domain of Information and Communication Technology. The legal situation in this area varies widely across Member States, particularly regarding standardisation of products. EC Mandate M/273 states that "Ideally all products and services should be accessible to 100% of the population" [4]. While it acknowledges that this is not practically possible, it goes on to provide a framework of dates by which Member States should have their legislation in order. By the end of 2001 Member States should have reviewed the relevant legislation dealing with the Information Society, with a view to ensuring their conformity with accessibility principles and accelerating standardisation processes.

The UK government have yet to undertake the review regarding the Information Society, and may be using the DDA to implement accessibility principles.

3.4 Standardisation

The European Commission has asked the European Standardisation Organisations (ESOs) to identify the standards needed to make the Information Society accessible to everyone, including those with special needs. The ESOs commissioned a report on Design-for-All and Assistive Technologies standardisation [5] and as a result are now looking into speech recognition and terminal access, and also the scientific application of knowledge about the capacities and limitations of users with the aim of making products, systems, services and environments safe, efficient and easy to use. The completed standards report for Assistive Technology Devices in Information and Communication Technology is due for publication on 30th May 2002.

3.5 Research

The new Community Framework Programme (FP6) for Research and Development [6] introduces important changes in the approach to EU funded research with relation to disabilities. One of the pivotal tenets of the framework describes the aim to focus research upon 'ambient intelligence systems offering access to the information society for all, whatever their age and situation, as well as interactive and intelligent systems for health and mobility…'.

One of the seven thematic areas of the FP6 Programme Consultation Meeting 1 [7] in May 2001 was 'Assistive Technologies (AT) for Persons with Disabilities'. This research area faces seven challenges including the removal of all barriers (e.g. technological, cultural, linguistic), Design-for-All and acceptance of AT products. The Consultation Meeting also recommended that the research conducted under FP6 'should target assistive systems… for disabilities'.

3.6 Web accessibility initiative and design-for-all (WAI-DA)

Another recommendation of the Mandate [4] is with regard to the Internet and e-Commerce, obliging all content providers to make their sites accessible to all by the usage of the WAI guidelines [8]. WAI-DA is a European Commission creation whose goal is to increase accessibility of the Web in EU Member States. This is to be achieved by complementing the work done at W3C-WAI (9) with educational and tools-based activities relevant to the European context. The project is due to end by 30th September 2002 and has three main objectives:

▶ to increase the extent of participation of individuals and organisations from EU Member States in international activities promoting Web accessibility,
▶ to increase awareness and implementation of the Web Content Accessibility Guidelines on Web sites within EU Member States, in order to increase the usability of European Web sites for people with disabilities,
▶ to increase the implementation of the Authoring Tool Accessibility Guidelines in Web authoring tools used in EU member states, so that people producing Web sites will more automatically be able to create accessible sites using these tools.

A resolution is due in summer 2002 by the Committee of the Regions, looking at ways of embedding the WAI guidelines into practice within Member States.

3.7 Education

Some of the recommendations to Member States from the Mandate [4] relevant to the advancement of people with disabilities in further and higher education include:

▶ to review standards and guidelines for user interface navigation in the office environment and adapt to the public/home/mobile environment,
▶ to develop a Code of Practice for minimum help facilities to be provided in relation to use of ICT services/products,
▶ to develop standards and guidelines for privacy and the security of information. To be accessible for all users/modalities,
▶ to elaborate standards on speech recognition, synthetic speech, consistency of user interface, standards for 'blind' navigation and its activation within Public Access Terminals. Elaborate standards on the interaction between the Public Access Terminal and different user or system assistive technology devices.

During 2002 the EC will support the creation of a Network of Centres of Excellence, at least one in each Member State, that will develop a European curriculum module in Design-for-All to train designers and engineers.

3.8 Tempus and Socrates

In the January 2000 communiqué "A New Generation of Programmes 2000-2006: Education, Training and Youth" [10], the European Commission declares that "efforts will be made under all programmes to include disadvantaged and disabled people". One programme that has particular relevance in this area is Socrates, which covers both school and further and higher education. In the new programme more emphasis will be placed on lifelong learning, the educational use of Information and Communication Technology, the dissemination of good practice and the inclusion of disadvantaged people.

The European Parliament [11] asserts that within Socrates "there is a need to promote active citizenship and to step up the fight against exclusion in all its forms… special attention should be given to persons with special needs". The objectives of Socrates include "to facilitate wide transnational access to educational resources in Europe while promoting equal opportunities throughout all fields of education" and "to encourage innovation in the development of educational practices and materials including, where appropriate, the use of new technologies". Two particular aspects of Socrates will be impacted by these recommendations: Erasmus, the transnational higher education scheme, and Minerva, which covers open and distance learning, Information and Communication Technologies in the field of education. Under the latter, "Community financial assistance may be awarded for projects and studies aimed at helping those involved in education to understand and exploit the innovative processes underway, in particular those relating to the use of ICT in teaching and learning, the development of innovative instruments and approaches, and methods for establishing criteria for quality assessment of ICT-based educational products and services".

The Tempus programme encourages exchanges in the field of higher education between UK institutions and those in Eastern Europe. With the imminent accession of many of these countries to the European Union, many will be seeking advice and assistance on accessibility issues. The links forged through the Tempus programme are likely to be a useful conduit for this information.

3.9 Conclusions

The FP6 Programme Consultation Meeting Report [7] estimated that by 2020 the proportion of EU citizens with a disability will have risen to 18% from today's 11%. It also recommended that 'by 2015 all European citizens with a disability should have the opportunity to use IT-based Assistive Technologies… at a level of expenditure that is affordable for them,' and that 'by 2015 all carers of disabled persons should have the opportunity to be supported and facilitated by IT-based applications, technologies and services'.
It is evident from the wide range of directives

emerging from Europe that the organisations of the European government are making every effort to support people with disabled people, both in terms of the production of assistive technologies (Design-for-All) and in the area of widening participation in education. If previous patterns are followed, it will not be long before Member States are required to integrate the principles contained within these directives into their own laws. It remains to be seen whether or not the UK will be among the first to adopt these principles and embed them into law, and into society in general. TechDis will be observing the output from Europe in this area and alerting the sector to resolutions that may affect the UK further and higher education sector.

3.10 References

[1] European Commission Information Society, eEurope Action Plan, available from: **http://europa.eu.int/ information_society/eeurope/ action_plan/index_en.htm**

[2] eGovernment Ministerial Conference, Ministerial Declaration, Brussels, 29th November 2001, available from: **http://europa.eu.int/ information_society/eeurope/egovconf/ documents/ Ministerial%20declaration%20English% 2029-11-01.pdf**

[3] Treaty of Amsterdam, Amending the Treaty on European Union, the Treaties Establishing the European Communities and Certain Related Acts, 2nd October 1997, available from: **www.w3.org/WAI/EO/EuropAmst.pdf**

[4] Design For All Project Team Executive Summary Report 15th May 2000, available from: **www.ict.etsi.org/activities/ Design_for_All/execsum.pdf**

[5] eEurope eAccessibility Report (November 2001), available from: **www.etsi.org/ literature/eEurope/E-Accessibility.pdf**

[6] Decision of the European Parliament and of the Council, COM (2001) 94 Final, 21st February 2001, 'Concerning the Multiannual Framework Programme 2002-2006 of the European Community for Research, Technological Development and Demonstration Activities aimed at contributing towards the creation of the European Research Area', available from: **http://ftp.cordis.lu/pub/ ist/docs/fp6finalversion.pdf**

[7] 6th Framework Programme 2002-2006

Programme Consultation Meeting 1 on
Technologies for Major Societal Challenges,
3 May 2001, available from:
**http://ftp.cordis.lu/pub/ist/docs/
pcm1final-report.pdf**

[8]   W3C Web Content Accessibility Guidelines
2.0, 24th August 2001, available from:
www.w3.org/TR/WCAG20/

[9]   W3C Web Accessibility Initiative, Design-
For-All Project Reference Guide, 8th
December 2000, available from:
www.w3.org/WAI/WAIDA/

[10] European Commission, Education, Training
and Youth – A New Generation of
Programmes (2000-2006), February 2000,
available from:
**http://europa.eu.int/comm/
education/newprogr/index.html**

[11] Decision No 253/2000/EC of the
European Parliament and of the Council, of
24th January 2000, establishing the second
phase of the Community action programme
in the field of education 'Socrates', available
from: **http://europa.eu.int/comm/
education/newprogr/
l00-28socratesii-en.pdf**

3 The role of assistive technologies in supporting student learning

Preface

Lawrie Phipps and **Allan Sutherland**

It is clear that assistive technologies have an important role to play in ensuring that inclusive learning is available to all students. However, there is such a bewildering array of assistive products on the market that it can be extremely difficult to know where to begin when trying to decide which item of assistive technology is most appropriate for individual students. In further and higher education specialist staff dedicated to provide support for disabled students are aware of these technologies and help students assess which of them suit their individual needs.

The TechDis Accessibility Database (TAD) can be used by student support staff to identify appropriate technologies and where to source them [1]. However, the TAD can provide insights about assistive technologies for all staff. It provides an online resource of information about assistive products that are available to assist disabled people. The resource is designed to provide information on assistive, adaptive and enabling technologies to the further and higher education sectors. However, it is important to note that the TAD is not intended to be used as a diagnostic tool. Users are encouraged to seek professional assistance with regard to the provision of support for disabled students and students with learning difficulties, and the appropriate use of the products and services held on the database.

The TAD contains more than 2,500 assistive technology products and can be browsed in three ways: by Product, Company and Learning and Teaching. The first two categories are, hopefully, self-explanatory but it may be helpful to say a little more about the Learning and Teaching approach. This has been designed to help those without specialist product knowledge to find assistive technologies that will be appropriate to the context in which they are learning or teaching. There are 14 sub-categories, as shown in Figure 1.

Staff involved in learning and teaching or learning technology can find useful information by browsing the TAD in the Learning and Teaching section. By selecting a disability and a Learning and Teaching category, the user will be presented with a list of products appropriate to both the disability and the educational context. This can be a very helpful opening gambit for a lecturer/teacher in a college or university who is interested in finding out how assistive technologies can work within their subject discipline.

Once the user has selected the relevant category, they are shown a list of products with descriptions, prices and supplier details. In many cases, they will also be provided with case studies that relate to the use of that product in a learning and teaching situation. For example, by selecting 'Blind/Visual Impairment' and 'Computer Laboratories' a user will see a list of more than 100 appropriate products and will also be able to find a number of linked case studies that will help them to consider the use of these technologies in their own disciplines. In this context, a user might find a case study on the FERL Web site [2] that "describes the experiences of Alan [not his real name], a school-leaver with fairly severe visual impairment, who embarked on a mathematics A-level course at Suffolk College." The user can also locate a series of links to 'How to' articles that provide practical advice on using the assistive technology as well as issues such as funding, accessibility and other types of equipment.

In this section, experienced practitioners explore the ways in which assistive technology can support students with visual impairment, hearing impairment, mobility impairment, or dyslexia. It is not possible for all of us in education to gain the same level of experience and knowledge but it is hoped that the TechDis Accessibility Database can at least provide a starting point.

[1]   TAD can be accessed at:
www.techdis.ac.uk/access.html

[2]   FERL is an information service for all staff
working within the Post Compulsory
Education sector. It aims to support
individuals and organisations in making
effective use of ICT through a Web based
information service, conferences,
publications and other events. The FERL
Web site can be found at: **www.ferl.org.uk**

Figure 1: options
when Browsing TAD
by Teaching and
Learning

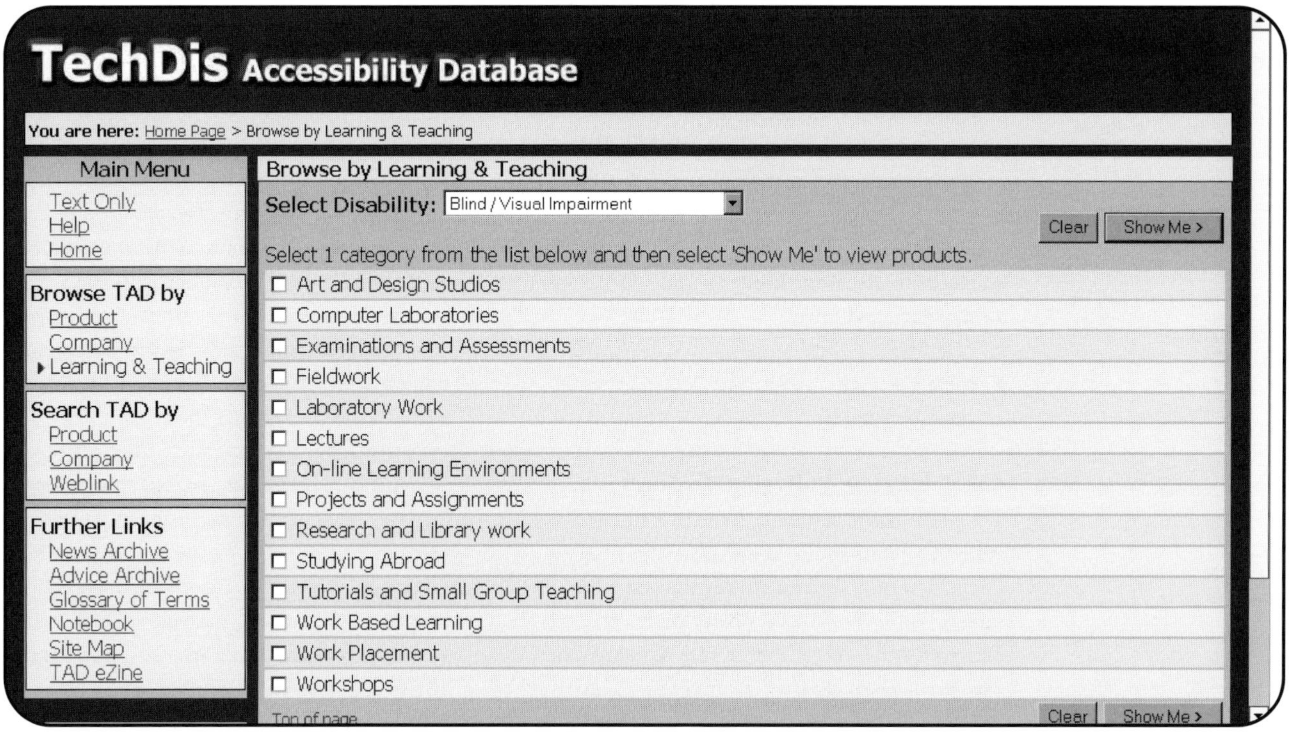

TechDis Accessibility Database

You are here: Home Page > Browse by Learning & Teaching

Main Menu	Browse by Learning & Teaching
Text Only Help Home	**Select Disability:** Blind / Visual Impairment ▾
	Clear Show Me >
Browse TAD by Product Company ▸ Learning & Teaching	Select 1 category from the list below and then select 'Show Me' to view products. ☐ Art and Design Studios ☐ Computer Laboratories ☐ Examinations and Assessments ☐ Fieldwork
Search TAD by Product Company Weblink	☐ Laboratory Work ☐ Lectures ☐ On-line Learning Environments ☐ Projects and Assignments
Further Links News Archive Advice Archive Glossary of Terms Notebook Site Map TAD eZine	☐ Research and Library work ☐ Studying Abroad ☐ Tutorials and Small Group Teaching ☐ Work Based Learning ☐ Work Placement ☐ Workshops
	Top of page Clear Show Me >

Chapter 4

Visual impairments and technology

Zoë Neumann, ICT Development Officer, Post 16 Education, RNIB

4.1 Introduction

This chapter will provide an overview of the main types of technologies that can be used by visually impaired learners. The value of such technologies will be illustrated using two case studies. Finally, barriers to the effective use of such technologies will be discussed with a focus on inclusive design principles.

4.2 Understanding the needs of students with a visual impairment

For blind and partially sighted students, access to courses in post-16 education is dependent on technology. The use of adaptations to personal computers for information retrieval, communication and written output as well as portable devices for taking and retrieving notes, have reduced the barriers to studying for blind and partially sighted students [1,2]. This has opened up enormous opportunities for people who have up to now been denied access to the vast majority of information in a format they can use effectively, let alone independently. The RNIB Technology Information Service provides a wide range of information on the kinds of technology that can help visually impaired people including detailed fact sheets, which you can find on their Web site [3]. The technology falls into six main areas:

▶ electronic Braille displays,
▶ electronic Reading aids,
▶ screen magnification,
▶ notetakers,
▶ speech output systems,
▶ video magnifiers.

4.2.1 Electronic Braille displays
These are tactile devices that are placed under a conventional computer keyboard, which enables the user to read the contents of the computer screen, by touch in Braille. The displays are designed with buttons and/or bars to enable the user to roam around the screen, reading whichever part they wish. To gain full access to computer software it may also be necessary to use a screen

reading programme. There are some purpose designed Notetakers on the market which have Braille displays and Braille keyboards and are designed as portable organizers with facilities for a diary, calculator, address book etc.

4.2.2 Electronic reading aids
Electronic Reading Aids are used to scan and translate printed text into a computer readable file. This can then be read with synthetic speech, magnification software or a Braille display. The reading aid consists of two main components:

▶ a scanner that is used to scan the text to be processed,
▶ recognition software that can be in the form of a printed circuit board or software stored on a disc.

Stand-alone reading aids are integrated units with a scanner, Optical Character Recognition software and speech software. The document is scanned and then read all by the same machine. These machines tend to be portable. PC based reading aids may use mainstream or specialised software but the software may not necessarily be integrated to include speech feedback. While this can be a cheaper option, PC based reading aids are not portable.

4.2.3 Screen magnification
Screen magnification software works by increasing the size of the image displayed on the screen. Therefore, only a portion of the original screen image can be seen at one time. Normally, the area around the cursor, mouse pointer or highlighted menu item is magnified. Some screen magnification programs now provide supportive speech output as well. Enlarging the text on the computer screen does restrict the amount of viewable area on the screen, but using a larger monitor in conjunction with screen magnification software can increase the viewing area on the screen. While there are specialised screen magnification software packages available, the Windows operating systems also include some screen enhancement features such as high contrast colour schemes, and larger font sizes.

4.2.4 Notetakers

There are four kinds of note-taking systems. Specialist electronic note-takers with Braille or Qwerty keyboard input, and speech and/or Braille output; small laptop computers running access software such as a screen reader; speech-based notetakers that are either tape-based (using cassette recorders) or digital (using Dictaphones or MiniDiscs) and Speech-based organizers, which are digital recorders with extra features such as diary and calculator.

4.2.5 Speech output systems

Typically a speech output system will consist of a speech synthesizer and screen reading software. A speech synthesizer, with a built in speaker and headphone socket, produces speech output from text sent to it from the screen-reading program installed on the computer. The speech synthesizer can be an external box, but it is usually a software application which uses a sound card as an output device. A screen-reading program sends screen text displayed on the screen to be spoken by a speech synthesizer. Common features include the ability to speak the full screen, a user defined area of the screen, a line, word, or individual letter.

4.2.6 Video magnifiers

Video magnifiers or CCTV act as a magnifying aid for people with some useful vision. Printed material and objects can be placed under a camera and the magnified image is displayed on a television screen or computer monitor. The majority of video magnifiers are intended for use on a desk or work surface. Most desktop magnifiers have a camera, which is in a fixed position some distance above the desktop. And a reading table or platform that rests on the desktop. The printed material is placed on the reading table, which can be moved left to right and backwards and forwards. A few desktop video magnifiers have a camera on an angle pose type stem, so there is some flexibility of position.

Within all areas of education and employment, assessment and training are fundamentals of gaining successful access to technology. Before embarking on a decision to purchase a particular device or application, it is necessary to determine the user's needs within the learning environment and therefore the role of Disability Student Advisor is essential. Understanding the different funding mechanisms for acquiring the specialist equipment and training are also essential.

4.3 Case studies of assistive technology in use

4.3.1 Using screen magnification software to assist in taking notes in lectures

Carl has some vision but is unable to access printed materials as quickly as his sighted counterparts. He uses a sophisticated screen magnification package and a scanner enabling him to take notes just as the others use pen and paper. Carl would not be able to use the laptop without screen magnification. The volume of reading that has to be done as part of Carl's course is immense. Within the screen magnification software is the option to use speech output. This allows him to have documents converted to speech by the laptop so that when his eyes get tired he can rely on speech and not use the magnification feature. Carl has supportive lecturers who provide handouts with enlarged text and accurate signposting in terms of reading materials. Carl scans the recommended texts and is then able to read them using text-to-speech or by printing out certain sections in a larger font. Materials are also sent to Carl using email and often in advance of a module so that he can prepare for the course. Carl also has a support worker to read for him, proof-read his assignments and access the library, paid for from his Disabled Students Allowance (DSA). The combination of assistive technology, a laptop computer and the human support enables Carl to do the same work as his sighted peers.

4.3.2 Using screen readers to facilitate access to the Internet and implications for Web design

Reading and navigating Web pages is a very different experience when the user can't see the screen. Instead of seeing the page as a whole, as the author intended, the user works through sequentially without any of the visual cues such as colour-contrast, font-size or position to tell them what is important and what may safely be skimmed. Additionally, if the page is split up into columns, frames or boxes, then in some cases the user may find that the text read by a screen reader (or Braille display) is garbled. This is because it may be reading two pieces of text that are unrelated and from two separate boxes on different parts of the screen. Sites which try to be helpful by putting all the most commonly used links at the top of every page force the reader to wade through those very same links on the reading of every page before the user comes to the principle material on the page. In some cases it will leave users wondering whether they are actually on the page they want, or if they have got stuck in an infinite loop. The Webaim Web site [4] provides several simulations, which provide the opportunity for users to experience a Web page as someone with a visual impairment might see it.

Most good screen readers work well with most Web browsers. Helpful commands include allowing the user to jump past a set of Web page links to the next piece of content, jump to the next frame within the Web page, or straight to the beginning of a form. It should also be possible to perform a search for particular items on the current page. To make sense of all but the simplest pages using a screen reader requires a good knowledge of the particular software being used, so training is required for both the designer and users.

Whatever technology is used a visually impaired user should always spend time developing effective methods for productive working, from getting familiar with one favourite search engine, to learning to save particularly relevant extracts for later use in Braille, E-text or large print.

4.4 Conclusions

When visually impaired learners have the necessary skills and technology to investigate and retrieve resources held in CD ROMs or the Internet, they have access to a wide range of curriculum materials that not only support their participation in the curriculum but also enrich and broaden their learning experience. Unfortunately, technology can still fail to deliver results if inclusive design principles are ignored. For example, software that is only highly graphical will not be read by a screen reader; there is a need for text to be integrated for the screen reader to make sense of screen content. Even software that looks very standard may be difficult to use if it offers poor keyboard control or the use of non-standard features or programming techniques.

Technology often fails to deliver results, but in the creation of e-learning environments, we are its driver. If we understand how the barriers to inclusion are being created in the profligacy of spending on, and acceptance of poor and narrow-minded design, then we can challenge our mindsets and apply consideration to the additional needs of disabled students. We have mechanisms to help us – inclusion policies, inspections, teaching standards and qualifications, The Special Educational Needs and Disabilities Act, The National Federation of Access Centres

(NFAC), The National Disability Team (NDT), The National Bureau for Students With Disabilities (SKILL) and so on [5,6,7]. What we need to implement is the cohesive sharing of practical experiences, effective commitment from education establishments, decisive procurement guidelines, awareness, training and dissemination. And this all needs to happen both within establishments and across the joining up of establishments.

4.5 Acknowledgements

This chapter was created using examples and contributions from the following people: Peter Bosher, Soundlinks; Seema Dass, RNIB; Richard Orme, RNIB; and extracts from:

[1]　Cain, S. and Orme, R. "Ensuring provision for students with a visual impairment using technology". Interactions, Volume 5, Number 3: **www.warwick.ac.uk/ETS/interactions**

[2]　"Accessing Technology. Using technology to support the learning and employment opportunities for visually impaired users", RNIB, **www.rnib.org.uk/technology**

[3]　RNIB Fact sheets available from **www.rnib.org.uk/technology**

4.6 References

[4]　**www.webaim.org/simulations/lowvision**

[5]　**www.nfac.org.uk**

[6]　**www.natdisteam.ac.uk**

[7]　**www.skill.org.uk**

Hearing disability and technology

Dr Mike Wald, Director, Southern Higher and Further Education Collaboration, University of Southampton

5.1 Introduction

This chapter will provide an overview of the main types of technologies that can be used to meet the needs of students with a hearing disability. The value of such technologies will be illustrated with a particular focus on how speech recognition can be used to assist teaching and learning. Finally, the importance of having an open dialogue between student and institution about how their needs can be met is highlighted.

5.2 Understanding the needs of students with a hearing disability

It is important to recognise that every student has his or her own individual needs. Although it is possible to 'measure' and describe a person's hearing ability in a variety of ways, understanding speech is a very complex process that can involve the eyes as well as ears and brain. It is therefore possible for a student with 'less' measured hearing to actually be able to understand what is being said better than another student who has 'more' measured hearing. Hearing disability can change over time, and can also involve tinnitus (hearing 'internally generated' sounds) or additional disabilities (e.g. visual).

British Sign Language (BSL) is a visual language, which does not use the same grammatical construction as English and is usually used without accompanying speech. As with any language it can be learnt 'informally' through communication with fluent users of the language or formally through classes. Various forms of sign language such as Sign Supported English (SSE) may be used with accompanying speech to help learn written and spoken English. Cued Speech can be used to aid lip reading and listening by using hand shapes to give visual cues for sounds.

The majority of deaf people were born to hearing parents and were taught at school without sign language support and so may not have learnt to use sign language. They use lip-reading combined with their hearing, aided by hearing aids or

cochlear implants (which stimulate nerves in the ear electrically). At school or college they may have received support from staff and fellow students and may have been taught in acoustically treated rooms. At university they may find it more difficult to cope using just hearing and lip reading due to background noise, reverberant rooms, poor lighting conditions and staff and students unused to talking to deaf students.

Some students who were born deaf or became deaf at a very young age may have less than perfect written and spoken English due to their lack of experience of reception of spoken English.

5.3 Accessibility of teaching and learning

Institutions need to think carefully about the structure of their courses, tutorial support, resources and staff development, as replacing large lectures and seminars by more accessible resource based learning using small tutorial groups and computer based learning can reduce the need for communication support. The provision of actual lecture and course notes etc. in advance can be a great help to the student and support worker, and providing these in electronic form may be the most flexible approach. The use of visual aids (e.g. PowerPoint slides) can also help support the understanding of spoken information. There are also a number of technological aids or services that the student can use to aid their hearing or facilitate access to information.

5.3.1 Radio aids
Many students will be using a hearing aid (or a cochlear implant) that, when combined with lip reading, can help them to understand what is being said. Digital hearing aid technology can provide a wider range of options to meet individual hearing needs in a wider range of situations than analogue aids. It is important to make the best use of hearing, and radio aids can improve the signal to noise ratio. Typically, the lecturer wears a radio microphone that transmits a high quality speech signal to the radio receiver worn by the student. This can work well in a

lecture type situation where most of the talking is done by the lecturer who can wear the radio microphone. However, if the student also needs to listen to students around them then they will need to also have their hearing aid's microphone switched on at the same time. In a seminar the radio microphone could be passed around from speaker to speaker or a second room microphone could be used. If in a class situation the lecturer is wandering around talking individually to other students without switching off the microphone their voice will continue to be sent inappropriately. If the student has a hearing aid with an appropriate socket on it, the signal from the radio receiver can be directly connected into the hearing aid by a lead, giving the best quality speech signal.

If the student's hearing aid does not have this socket a 'neck loop' can be used which can be worn around the neck and plugged into the radio receiver. This is like a miniature loop system and so the student can switch his hearing aid to the loop T position to pick up the signal. This gives a more consistent signal than a fixed room loop while being entirely portable from room to room. A 'loop' is a loop of wire that is used to transmit an amplified signal to be picked up by the hearing aid when switched to the T position. Loop systems can normally only significantly improve the signal to noise ratio if they use a directional microphone that is closer to the speaker's mouth than the hearing aid microphone. Infra red systems, while capable of providing high quality signals, tend to be more expensive, not portable and do not cope well with direct sunlight.

It is important that rooms and amplification system acoustics are well designed. Using well positioned, multiple loudspeakers can often be helpful. Portable sound field amplification systems are available and may help students unable to use a radio aid or loop system. Equipment that has a sound output (e.g. TV, video, computer etc.) may be able to be connected to a hearing aid rather than the student having to use amplified headphones or loudspeaker output. The sound output could also be fed into the auxiliary input of a radio aid.

5.3.2 Captioning/Subtitles
Ensuring that information provided in audio format (e.g. speech) on all media (e.g. television, videos, CD-ROMs, DVD, Web pages, VLEs) is also provided in a visual medium (i.e. BSL or text) will ensure it is accessible for students. If the captioned audio needs to be synchronised to

visual information then commercial subtitling/captioning rates are high if work is done to broadcast guidelines where the alternate visual form is carefully designed (e.g. position, speed of information etc.). A cheaper, simpler approach sufficient to support students in FE and HE could often be undertaken in house. Many TV programmes are subtitled for deaf people and can be recorded and replayed using available technology.

5.3.3. Sign language interpreting
Students fluent in sign language may choose interpreters as the best and most flexible means of support. However the shortage of trained and qualified sign language interpreters may result in students using those with lesser experience and qualifications.

Although technologies are no substitute for the versatility of a skilled human interpreter, it is possible to provide automatic computer generated 3D animated Signed English from electronic text although satisfactory 'translation' to British Sign Language will be much more difficult to achieve. It is also technically possible to automatically 'translate' text to sign language using stored sign language video clips. This can be combined with speech recognition to first automatically transcribe the speaker's words into text and then automatically turn the speaker's words into sign language. However this would be 'word for word signing' rather than BSL, although there is research currently underway on how to translate text into BSL. There is no simple way to automatically translate sign language into written text, although it is technically possible to look up signs in a visual dictionary to find the text 'equivalent'.

Sign Language Skills Development CD-ROMs are available to help develop knowledge of sign language.

5.3.4 Recording of lectures
Digital audio recording of lectures can allow the lectures to be transcribed after the event, although information that had been presented visually will not be represented unless digital video recordings are also made.

5.3.5 Real time verbatim transcription system
A phonetic transcription system such Palantype, or Stenotype requires a specially trained, skilled person to operate it and allows an accurate verbatim real time text transcription of what is being said at speeds of up to 240 words per

minute. It uses a special phonetic keyboard and a skilled operator using this technology can produce an accurate, readable, real time text display for a deaf person to enable them to follow live speech. Since no summarising is occurring the operator does not require subject knowledge, although any 'new' words or names need to be added to the system's dictionary. The requirement for a highly skilled and trained operator, also in demand for legal services and real time subtitling of television programs, influences the cost and availability of this service.

5.3.6 Note-taking support

It is difficult for students to lip-read or watch an interpreter and take notes at the same time and so notetakers are often required. Notetakers can record both textual and graphical information on paper. Some rephrasing and summarising is required by the operator and so quality is dependent on how well the operator can understand and summarise the information. If a student who does not use sign language support is actually having difficulty following what is being said, they might also wish to refer to the notes as they are being written.

5.3.7 Portable note-taking devices

If students can touch-type it is possible to use a portable note-taking device to help take notes in class while being able to look at and lip-read the speaker, or watch the interpreter without having to look down at their notes. The device needs preferably to be small, light, with a long battery life and a good keyboard. Devices that just store the text, which can be later transferred to a computer, are normally cheaper, smaller and lighter than laptop computers. It is also possible to learn to use special keyboards that use combinations of keys pressed simultaneously.

5.3.8 Electronic note-taking

Software to help with electronic note-taking can allow people with audio typing skills to type faster by using expanded abbreviations, although not at real time transcription rates. As with note-taking on paper, some rephrasing and summarising is required by the operator and so quality is dependent on how well the operator can understand and summarise the subject. Some systems allow the student to add their own notes as well. Since less training is required for the operator than for Palantype this service may be cheaper. Note-taking using pen and paper allows for diagrams to be included, which is more difficult to achieve electronically. Speech recognition can be used to assist electronic note-taking, by

allowing the notetaker to shadow or repeat or summarise what is being said in the class/lecture room at faster than typing speeds. If the notetaker is in the classroom, a special 'mask' that covers the notetaker's mouth will be required to reduce the sound of the notetaker speaking, which may be a distraction to others nearby and also keep extraneous noises from affecting the speech recognition. This problem does not occur if the notetaker is using speech recognition while operating remotely via telephone or network.

5.3.9 Remote real time communication support

Providing transcription or interpreting services remotely could reduce the cost because the person providing the service does not have to travel to the lecture. It would therefore be possible to pay for a shorter session and have the choice of employing people from a much wider geographical area who may have more appropriate skills and knowledge. High quality video and audio using ISDN lines or a fast computer network is at present required for remote sign language interpreting while it is possible to provide remote text transcription services using standard telephone lines, data networks, or mobile phones. As videophones become more commonly available they will also help students who use sign language or lip-reading to communicate at a distance in their preferred way.

5.3.10 Text communication

Students who cannot use standard telephones require Textphones in key areas (e.g. accommodation, reception, switchboard, library, medical centre, computer services, counselling service, student welfare offices). It is possible for a textphone user to communicate with a person using an ordinary telephone using a relay service.

Real time text chat over networks can also allow text communication for individuals and groups, however unlike fully duplex textphones, chat systems usually require the user to complete their communication before it is sent and appears on the other person's computer. This prevents natural 'interruptions', which can speed up conversation and also creates temporal interruptions, which can slow down the conversation and confuse the participants, particularly if many users are chatting simultaneously.

Both email and SMS messaging are valuable means of communication between both deaf and hearing students. Fax can also be useful.

5.4 Using speech recognition to assist teaching and learning

Current speech recognition applications are relatively inexpensive and capable of accurate and fast responses on standard computers for normal rates of speech, with minimal training of the system to the speaker's voice or training of the user of the technology. Speaker-independent systems that require no enrolment/training may be available in the near future.

Staff and students may have preferences regarding whether and when they find the spoken or written forms of language easier or more useful for teaching and learning. Text to speech applications can automatically change text into speech while speech recognition technology can be used to automatically change speech into text. Whether speech recognition technology can understand a deaf student's speech can only be established by trial. Speech recognition can be used by academic staff to produce teaching materials and by students for producing coursework and notes. Speech-recognition can also be used to replace the keyboard for those with a physical disability or to help prevent, or support those who already have, Repetitive Strain Injury (RSI) or work-related upper limb disorders (WRULD).

5.4.1 Real time text transcription in lectures

Speech-recognition can be used for providing real time text transcription in lectures to provide a text display of what is being spoken as well as a verbatim transcript for later reference. To achieve a similar result without the technology would involve the use of expensive, highly trained real-time speech to text reporters who are in great demand for court reporting and real time subtitling of television programmes. Standard speech recognition applications require the user to dictate punctuation to break up the text into 'readable' chunks. The Liberated Learning Project uses an application that provides a readable display from the normal speech of lecturers without requiring the dictation of punctuation. Real time speech to text transcription can assist deaf students who find it difficult to follow the lecturer through hearing alone. It can also be of benefit for students or lecturers whose first language is not English and when there are poor acoustics (e.g. excessive reverberation or background noise or too quiet speech). In addition to deaf students who need to watch to lip-read or follow a sign-language interpreter, the

automatic production of a verbatim transcript for later reference can assist any students who find it difficult to take notes during a lecture, for example dyslexic students, visually impaired students, or students who have a physical disability affecting writing or typing. In addition many students who have no disability or learning difficulty find it difficult to take notes at the same time as listening, watching and thinking. Speech-recognition can also be used to support distance learning by providing automatic speech to text transcription for online text chat, email and video or audio-conferencing.

5.5 Technology to improve speech and listening skills

Software and hardware is available to help improve speech intelligibility and develop listening skills, although this is normally used in conjunction with professionals trained in these fields.

5.5.1 Wireless video camera to aid lip-reading

A wireless video camera worn round the neck of the person speaking could provide a clear large video image of the speaker's face even if the speaker turns away, is at a distance or has their face obscured by other students etc.

5.5.2 Aids to spoken communication

Communication aids can provide text or spoken output for students who have speech that is difficult to understand, although just because the technology exists, does not mean students will wish to use it. They may for example prefer to use less conspicuous 'low technology' solutions such as paper and pen.

5.6 Assessment, exams and quality of written and spoken English

Some students, who were born deaf or became deaf when very young, may have less than perfect written and spoken English due to their lack of experience of reception of spoken English. The use of word processors with support utilities such as ideas planning (e.g. mind mapping), dictionary, thesaurus, and spelling and grammar checking can be helpful. Institutions need to consider carefully their policy on the use of technology in exams so as not to disadvantage students who would normally depend on such technology for coursework.

5.7 Health and safety

Students may not always be aware of auditory fire or smoke alarms, particularly if they are working alone or in noisy areas. Visual alarms and vibrating pager systems can help. Loud, visual or vibrating alarms can also be installed in accommodation to alert deaf students to alert when a doorbell, telephone or alarm rings.

5.8 Conclusions

Institutions can provide technology, based on knowledge and information about what that technology can in theory achieve or has in practice achieved for others. Institutions can also do a great deal to ensure their policies and practice assists technology in helping removing barriers to learning and participation. However, since only the individual student can decide whether any particular technology is appropriate to meet their particular individual needs it is important for student and institution to discuss these needs and how they can best be met. It is also important to discuss what the student can provide (e.g. through the Disabled Students Allowance) and what the institution can provide.

Explanatory note on terminology: there are many different terms that can be used to describe hearing disability (e.g. deaf, hard of hearing, hearing impaired) and although it is recognised that individuals may have strong personal preferences, to aid readability the term 'deaf' in this paper will denote 'hearing disability'. Also to aid readability the term 'students' throughout this chapter will refer to 'students with a hearing disability' or 'hearing disabled students' unless explicitly otherwise stated.

5.9 Resources

[1]   Frank W. Lovejoy Symposium, Applications of Automatic Speech Recognition with Deaf and Hard of Hearing People Rochester, NY: April 10-11, 1997, available from: **www.rit.edu/flewcncp/Lovejoy.html**

[2]   Mike Wald, Developments In Technology To Increase Access To Education For Deaf And Hard Of Hearing Student, Proceedings of CSUN "Technology and Persons with Disabilities" Conference, March 20-25, 2000, available from: **www.csun.edu/ cod/conf2000/proceedings/ 0218Wald.html**

[3]   Mike Wald, Developments In Mobile Telecommunications Technology To Increase Access To Education For Deaf And Hard Of Hearing Students, Conference Proceedings "International Mobile Telecommunications Seminar", Potsdam Germany, June 6-7, 2000, available from: **www.soton.ac.uk/flshec/ mobiletelecommunications.html**

[4]   Internet Resources for Deaf and Hard of Hearing Students, available from: **www.lisa.sbu.ac.uk/deafinitely_able**

[5]   Liberated Learning Project: (Using speech recognition to create a learning environment free of barriers), available from: **www.liberatedlearning.com**

[6}   RNID fact sheets and leaflets, available from: **www.rnid.org.uk/html/ info_factsheets.htm**

[7]   Mike Wald, Southern Higher Education Consortium: Discussion Paper 2: Supporting Students with Hearing Disabilities, available from: **www.soton.ac.uk/flshec/ deafdiscussionpaper.htm**

[8]   Gary Bunt, Widening Access in Philosophical and Religious Studies for Deaf and Hearing-Impaired Students, available from: **www.prs-ltsn.leeds.ac.uk/access/ discussions/hearing1.html**

Chapter 6

Dyslexia and technology

EA Draffan, TechDis Accessibility Database

6.1 Introduction

This chapter will provide an overview of how assistive technologies can assist dyslexic students in five main teaching and learning situations: listening; reading; organisation and memory; written language and calculations. The rationale for how these technologies can help will be given along with examples of products that are frequently used by dyslexic students.

6.2 Understanding the needs of dyslexic students

Dyslexia is often described as a specific learning difficulty and as such it reveals itself in many different ways. Dyslexia is not just a difficulty with words. Accordingly the use of technology that only helps with spelling and reading may not address the whole range of specific learning difficulties. Some concerns that those with dyslexia cope with on a daily basis include:

▶ short-term memory or working memory inadequacies, resulting in information, whether presented in a text format or spoken, often requiring repetition or reviewing,

▶ auditory processing skills where the combinations of sounds, words and phrases cause confusion and do not necessarily help with spelling or understanding,

▶ visual processing skills where the speed of interpreting text may be slower than expected and copying, for instance notes, can prove unhelpful as inaccuracies and missed sections may render the task ineffective,

▶ hand-eye coordination, which can affect writing skills,

▶ poor time management, organisational skills and concentration, which cause undue stress and are often the characteristics noticed by others.

However, Information Communication Technology (ICT) can provide immediate feedback, automaticity and encouragement as abilities improve through repetition of skills and processes. It has been said that by learning to touch-type a person with dyslexia may often be able to spell words that they are unable to write by hand,

because the process of letter positioning and formation becomes less of a concern. The fact that text and graphics can be constantly modified and neat presentation of work is no longer an issue, may also be beneficial. Learning with the aid of computers can be a multisensory experience tapping into many different learning styles and for the dyslexic, technology can provide sound through text to speech as well as graphics and animation to enhance written work.

Assistive technology at a post-16 level is designed to provide compensatory strategies, not correction or training to encourage better phonological awareness or visual discrimination or even to teach spelling rules. It should encourage independence and enhance literacy, numeracy and organisational skills. However, it may not always include a computer or high-tech solution, as even the humble Post-it Note or piece of coloured paper may prove a more efficient reminder compared to the handheld device that requires a rechargeable battery.

6.2 Teaching and learning situations

Every learning and teaching situation requires a variety of skills so for ease of allocating different types of technology, the areas covered are listening, reading, organisation and memory, written language, and simple calculations.

6.2.1 Listening

Recording lectures and tutorials can be very helpful for those who need to re-listen to what has been said in order to make accurate notes and to perhaps discuss the content with others at a later date. However, providing handouts at the beginning of a tutorial or lecture can be the most helpful strategy since the dyslexic student can then concentrate on what the speaker is saying without having to be concerned with full note-taking.

The types of audio recorders on offer vary from the MiniDisc with around 150 minutes in mono mode to standard recorders with 60-90 minute tapes. External microphones can improve the quality of the recording and are particularly important in lecture theatres where the recorder needs to be placed as near to the speaker as possible. Micro and mini cassette recorders are helpful for personal notes and all machines should have digital counters or a method for noting where important items can be found on the disks or tapes. Digital recorders can be used to take in the user's own speech to be converted at a later date into some speech recognition packages via a transcription facility such as that available in Dragon Dictate Naturally Preferred or IBM Via Voice mobile. This type of recording with text output is being trialled in some institutions as a method of providing instant notes. This is also possible with the provision of electronic whiteboards with laptops and printers.

Transcribing machines are available for micro, mini and standard tape recorders and these can be used with a foot switch, which is very helpful for the touch typist writing up lecture notes or a pre-recorded assignment.

Listening to speakers through a pair of head-phones, using the amplification system in a similar way to those with a hearing impairment, can be supportive for those who are distracted by extraneous sounds. This can also help to enhance the clarity of some speakers. In all cases it is essential that those giving lectures and tutorials are aware that some students may have auditory perceptual difficulties and/or short term memory problems and will be asking for items to be repeated.

If a student can touch-type faster than they can write they may find that it is possible to listen to lectures and use a lightweight portable keyboard such as an AlphaSmart or Calcuscribe in order to make notes. Handheld Personal Digital Assistants (PDAs) can often be used with additional keyboards and some are clamshell in design like the HP Jornada 720 with inbuilt keyboards. Text held on all the devices mentioned can be synchronised with a computer and provide a speedy way of reviewing what has been said.

6.2.2 Reading

Reading forms a major part of most curricular activities whether from the Internet, journals and books or lecture notes and handouts. For the student with dyslexia this can be a daunting part of a course if their reading speed is, for instance, half that of most other students. This may not be the only problem, there may also be the issues of remembering what has been written when the mechanics of working through the text has taken

so long and, because reading is such an effort, vocabulary levels are poor so comprehension suffers. Using dictionaries is hard work navigating lists of alphabetical words and finding the correct one when sequencing and spelling are weak, makes the task even more time wasting.

Coloured overlays, glasses and lamps with coloured films have all been found to help those with poor visual processing skills that may not necessarily be linked to visual acuity. Poor visual processing can result in tracking problems, reversing letters, failing to notice whole words, jumping lines of text and skipping sections. When using a computer, changing the desktop colours can help, as well as finding the most comfortable font, spacing and column widths.

Listening to books through tapes and discs is another way of assisting in the task of reading but this does not easily allow for reviewing, working back through small sections or highlighting key points unless the text is available at the same time. If the text is available a scanner with Optical Character Recognition (OCR) can help, with the text being read back through synthesised speech (e.g. TextHelp Read and Write or Write Outloud). The voices are improving. For example, Lernhout and Hauspie's 'Real Speak' no longer sounds quite so mechanical and there are pitch and rate controls with most programs. The speed of reading may often be faster than is normally possible by the reader when coping with just print versions. This can even result in increased understanding. Programs like Wynn, WordSmith and Kurzweil 3000/1000 allow for the page to be scanned with pictures and text remaining in the original format, providing the multisensory approach. Fonts and colours of the text and background can be changed to suit the user, pictures enhanced, notes can be added, text can be highlighted and there is a dictionary for checking word meanings.

Reading and scanning pens can also be used in libraries or when on the move, to take in short amounts of text that can be read back or to take in one word so that the meaning can be read back through the pen's dictionary (e.g. Quicktionary reading pen). The scanning pens operate in conjunction with a computer and some have diaries and address books such as the C-pens.

Online libraries with academic texts have been increasing in recent years and the files can be downloaded in various formats. Handheld devices such as the portable Palm, Pocket PC and e-

Bookman series have meant that it is possible to read digital text format on the move, sometimes with text to speech. Microsoft Reader can be downloaded to a computer, to provide a free text to speech program, dictionary and highlighting for certain file formats and there are many other basic screen reading programs like 'ReadPlease'. These types of screen reading programs tend to only read the text in a window and do not read menus or dialog boxes as would be expected for those who require support for visual difficulties. Microsoft Windows 2000/xp and Mac systems also have their own basic text to speech programs – Narrator and PlainTalk.

6.2.3 Organisation and memory

Many office software packages come with helpful scheduler systems that can be used to remind the user about events and reminders will appear at set times on the desktop or will sound an alarm. These packages also have contact files and both scheduler and address list can be updated from certain personal digital assistants (PDAs). However, these devices tend to follow a hierarchical pattern of reminders with linear layout. This may not be the best way of working for those with dyslexia. It does not compare that favourably to the brightly coloured piece of paper placed in a prominent position on the way out of the house or a series of Post-it Notes that can be shuffled to help organise thought processes.

It may be that a combination of technologies and paper-based ideas are needed to help with time management and organisational skills. This may be particularly important when planning assignments. The schedulers can be set up to appear on opening the computer, with highlighted text and reminder dates and times, whilst the organisational tools can include graphical brainstorming programs like Inspiration, MindManager or Thinksheet. These programs can be used in conjunction with word-processing programs but all work in slightly different ways so the user can choose which they prefer. Pictures, flow charts and spider grams are all available and text can be imported or exported along with Web pages and quotes from other sources.

When it comes to keeping notes and finding them again it may be helpful to use a free-form database within the scheduler/diary or Personal Information Manager (PIM). These programs allow the user to type in one or even half a word and the search system brings up any links to that word. Databases tend to be built in a rigid, hierarchical structure where each item of information must fit into a

field, the field must be defined in advance, and the data cannot vary from the field as defined in any way. However, the notes held on a PDA or computer memo or task program or 'To do' list can be sorted, dated and stored for future use with no more than a title field required with the details in any text form.

6.2.4 Written language

Written language is more ordered and also less prone to error than spoken language and assignments, projects, essays and examinations are expected to be presented in this format. Nevertheless, it may be that a more graphical or multimedia method would suit many dyslexic students. Writing for two or more hours in a script that deteriorates over time can prove very stressful in an examination setting. Other methods for tackling these educational requirements may provide more rewarding results – for instance, the use of technologies such as video, computer generated or graphical presentations and laptops in examinations.

The English writing system has so many exceptions to letter-to-sound correspondence rules that it appears chaotic to someone with dyslexia who may require a definitive framework from which to work. "The spoken word 'fish' could be spelled 'ghoti' – using the gh from tough, the o from women, and ti from nation. There are positional constraints, however, that would prevent 'fish' from being written in this way, but it illustrates the irregularity of the English language. In English, 40 or so phonemes (speech sounds) are represented with 26 characters. Some phonemes are represented by more than one character (c and k, j and g, f and ph), some represent more than one phoneme (g in great and general, c in cat and city, f in first and of), and others make no sound at all (k in knight, b in lamb). Within this apparent chaos there are rules however that govern pronunciation." From this chaos order can come with the help of spellcheckers but they do not always fulfil their job description.

Many dyslexics complain that the spellchecker has not helped when they are proof reading their documents and this is because they may spell in a way that is different from the database supplied with the spellchecker program. It may be using frequent typos as in Microsoft Word or mainly phonetic errors as in most spellcheckers designed specifically for those with dyslexia. These systems do not find the missed word, misplaced phrase or bizarre spelling that looked like a suitable word when it was written but turns out to be a malapropism.

Spellcheckers are incorporated within most word processing packages and as separate programs such as TextHelp Read and Write, SpellCatcher, Write Outloud and many free or shareware spell-checking programs can be downloaded from the Internet. Handheld Pocket spellcheckers vary in size and are available with a variety of dictionaries including Collins. Some have thesaurus, dictionary and homophone facilities, the more expensive versions have speech and larger screens with bigger keys.

CD-ROM and online dictionaries are available for many subjects and the contents can be read with a text to speech program. This can help the user understand the meaning of complex words but there are times when the pronunciation may not be very accurate. There are a series of talking dictionaries that have digitised speech and all the words are pronounced clearly in male or female voices, for example the Concise Oxford Dictionary. Word prediction programs can help in some circumstances but can also slow the quick typist. The user has to be able to choose from a selection of predicted words based on the letters first typed in a word, the frequency of use and position within a sentence. Each word or phrase is entered by using a single number or function key. This may not always be easy if the list is long and on the screen when the typist is looking at the keyboard. However, these programs may be of more assistance when the word lists are tailor made for the user and contain topic specific items or the user has problems thinking of particular words but knows the first letter. The list also allows the user to see the correct spelling and this in itself may be beneficial in the learning process.

Speech or voice recognition software, that allows the user to dictate text into the computer, has developed rapidly and training times have been cut drastically on powerful machines with ample memory, a good head microphone and clear continuous speech. In fact clarity is not such an issue if the sound combinations made are similar whenever the user tries the package. The problem is that the user also needs to know how to dictate and have some understanding of punctuation and written language sentence constructions which, as mentioned at the beginning of this section, are different from spoken language. It may be that the software is used for the initial drafts and note making and then the keyboard is used for the final stages. Accurate proof reading is essential as spelling mistakes rarely if ever appear but words that make no sense within a sentence can be missed because they may sound similar to the intended word when the screen reader is being used. Training is essential if full use of all the commands and shortcuts are to be learnt and tips are tried before frustration and valuable time is lost. Dragon Dictate Naturally Speaking and IBM ViaVoice are the two main packages in use; the latter is available for Mac as well as PC.

6.2.5 Calculations

Those students who have to cope with statistics or various calculations within their courses often struggle initially with the concepts but once these have been learnt it may be the simple tasks that are required to work out the sums that cause problems. Sequencing errors, transposing or reversing numbers, jumping lines of calculations or missing sections are often highlighted as issues. Using spreadsheets with text to speech can help as can talking handheld calculators.

The usual small handheld calculators or complex graphical ones used by students sometimes fail to help those with dyslexia because the text is too small, the small screens unclear and the left to right layout unhelpful. Computer based onscreen calculators often allow for font and background colour changes and even a descending layout for sums and a talking mode. There are also several free talking calculators that can be downloaded (e.g. SmartSum).

6.3 Conclusion

All assistive technology has to be well matched to the user and, as there is such a wide choice available it is important to understand the difficulties that each individual encounters in a teaching and learning situation. Time can be wasted if the technologies hinder learning and cause demoralisation as failure sets in. Training and evaluating the continued use of the technologies should ensure greater success. Although not strictly related to technology and dyslexia, it is also vital to think about the environment within which the tools are to be used. A comfortable height adjustable chair and large table with room for files can help concentration; good lighting that does not cause screen reflections can help reading. A clean screen, comfortable keyboard with wrist rests and mouse rests all go towards a more ergonomically friendly work setting. Using a toolkit made up of a series of portable devices such as recorders and lightweight keyboards as well as the multimedia computer with its word processing packages, organisational tools and text to speech as well as perhaps speech recognition, can make all the difference to a student with dyslexia. But the human support that teaching staff, the learning resource teams, student services, assistive technology centres and other bodies can supply remains paramount.

6.4 Resources

[1] Gay, G. (2001), Learning to learn, available from: **http://snow.utoronto.ca/Learn2/ introll.html**

[2] Hammond, J. and Hercules, F., Understanding Dyslexia; An Introduction for Dyslexic students in Higher Education, The Glasgow School of Arts, available from: **www.shefc.ac.uk/content/library/ dyslexia.html**

[3] Higgins, K. and Boone, R. (1997), Technology for Students with Learning Disabilities Pub Pro-ed. Austin. CD-ROM of the text available with the book.

[4] Singleton, C.H. (1999), Dyslexia in Higher Education: policy, provision and practice. (The Report of the National Working Party on Dyslexia in Higher Education), Hull, University of Hull for the Higher Education Funding Council for England

All products mentioned, with descriptions and supplier's addresses can be found on the TechDis Accessibility Database at: **www.techdis.ac.uk**

Physical disability and technology

Philip Henderson, Treloar Trust

7.1 Introduction

The term 'physical disability' describes a broad range of disabilities, syndromes and conditions. A large number of these can affect cognitive function (sometimes known as 'hidden disabilities') creating more challenging hurdles than purely finding solutions to a lack of physical ability. It is outside the bounds of this chapter to discuss disability in greater detail, but it is worth bearing in mind that a different approach may be required depending on whether a student has been disabled from birth or later in life. Similarly, awareness of whether a condition is stable, degenerative or with the potential to improve should affect the approach and expectation. Needless to say age appropriateness is paramount.

Frequently the term 'technology' is assumed to refer to high-tech (computer based) equipment, yet, in this context, it includes any intervention taking advantage of science and therefore can encompass the use of low-tech products as basic as masking tape. This chapter will provide an overview of the range of hardware and software technology that may facilitate access to the curriculum for physically disabled students.

7.2 Provision of technology

Technology, especially computer-based technology, is constantly evolving with new products appearing all the time. Some are very good, whereas others have questionable application. Disabled users are often reliant on other people to maintain these products on their behalf. Where educational institutions are committed to supporting disabled students, the delivery, staffing, training and technical support must be carefully thought through.

Technological products fall into two categories: those designed for the general public that are mass-produced, or those designed specifically for disabled users being more robust, but costing proportionally more due to the numbers made. In some cases students are solely reliant on specific technologies, such as communication devices. It is crucial that a system to provide repair and maintenance within acceptable timescales is in place.

Although this chapter may seem biased towards PCs (they are the most common platform, by far) much of the content is relevant to other operating systems, even if the choices of software are limited.

7.3 Ergonomics

The responsibility of health and safety falls on the employer to ensure employees are not at risk when using information and communication technology (ICT) equipment. Although this legislation does not directly apply to educational establishments with regard to students, common sense states that by addressing these issues problems will not occur or be exacerbated. This burden usually falls on the teaching staff; therefore it is important that they have a good understanding of health and safety issues associated with the use of ICT.

Further information on this and related subjects should be available in all educational institutions. Clear guidance can be obtained from the BECTa Web site [1]. Although this information is aimed specifically at schools, the content is perfectly valid for all ages.

Obviously wheelchair users need access to all rooms yet manoeuvring space within each room is often overlooked, especially where other students are working. As powered wheelchairs develop and become more sophisticated giving greater independence so they get bigger and require more space to turn.

Posture and positioning is often the difference between a disabled person accessing equipment or not. With this in mind, a little thought to room layout, desk arrangement and positioning of equipment goes a long way to providing a more accessible environment.

7.4 Hardware: low-tech equipment

There is no point providing complicated technology to solve problems where simpler solutions will work, often in a more sustainable way. Pen grips for people with poor hand function come in a variety of shapes and sizes. Writing slopes improve hand function by creating a rest for the forearm while raising the work so as to save the user looking down. Both copy holders and bookstands are simple items that can make a big difference in the long term. The addition of a copyholder will not only help keep surfaces free of clutter but reduce the need to look down, maintaining a better neck posture. Dycem mats are effective in preventing objects sliding across a table. Creative use of everyday items including masking tape, 'BluTack', 'Post-It Notes', etc. can be extremely useful.

Mobile arm supports are sometimes recommended for people with little strength in their upper body. They should be set up by an experienced person, preferably an occupational therapist, to ensure correct posture is maintained and no referred problems are created.

7.5 Hardware: high-tech equipment

7.5.1 Input devices

Generally, specialist keyboards perform the identical function to a standard model but are designed to fulfil a specific requirement, for example they may be much smaller reducing the range needed to select all the keys.

Most keyboards, whether large or small, use individual keys providing tactile, and in many cases, audible feedback. Others have a smooth membrane surface, either with a fixed key layout or an overlay system where the arrangement and design can be changed in seconds by swapping a flexible sheet on the front of the keyboard.

Layout of keys may be different to the commonly used 'Qwerty' arrangement, usually to reduce the effort of moving around the keyboard while typing. This is often referred to as 'frequency of use', where commonly used keys are grouped together, with the lesser-used keys at the edges of the keyboard.

Some keyboards feature the ability to control the mouse cursor on screen giving the user reasonably good access. This method is not able to reproduce the fluid movement that other more traditional pointing devices allow.

7.5.2 Pointing devices

The mouse remains the primary method of moving a cursor around the screen. Current incarnations afford much more in the way of ergonomics, additional buttons and wheels. They are no doubt more comfortable to use and increase efficiency, especially when used with applications that take advantage of these features. Optical mice provide a maintenance free device, very useful where the user lacks the dexterity to remove the mouse ball and clean it. Cordless models also have their place, removing the problem of cables getting caught on other desk-based objects causing resistance to movement.

Students who are unable to control a mouse sufficiently may use a joystick, trackerball or touch pad. Leading mouse manufacturers produce a wide range of trackerballs, aimed mainly at the mainstream market for those wishing to prevent or reduce the effects of repetitive strain injury (RSI), and these are often useful for users with other physical disabilities. Touch pads seem to be the norm on the current generation of laptop computers and external models are available for use with desktop PCs. These require little physical effort to move the cursor and are frequently recommended for students who lack strength and have limited range of movement. Joysticks are usually used by students with poorer dexterity.

Many pointing devices have additional buttons. These can enable functions such as a drag, double click and in cases are programmable. Some devices have a speed control giving a wider range of cursor movement speed than available through the operating system control panel.

7.5.2 Alternative input methods

Where a student is unable to operate even a specialist keyboard and pointing device there are a number of options available; some are listed below.

Switches: These come in all shapes and sizes and are generally used when other input methods are not viable. They can be operated by any part of the body and positioning is often critical. Due to the fact that switch software requires scanning of some sort it is inherently slow. Although there are many software packages specifically created for switch users, full independence is only available from the use of a keyboard emulator (see section 7.6.5).

Head mice: These systems enable the cursor to be controlled by movement of the head with software allowing the user access to all common mouse functions. By using a keyboard emulator a user can work independently as long as they have fine head control.

Voice recognition: Since the mid 90s the development of voice recognition systems has opened up new possibilities to some disabled users. The newer continuous speech systems have a particular application for dyslexic users (see Chapter 6), whereas the original discrete system, where the user has to say each word separately, includes good mouse control and is often more appropriate for severely physically disabled people. These systems require a large input of time from both the student in terms of training the voice and a trainer to ensure the system is set up for optimum performance. Remember voice recognition may be the only method of input for a physically disabled user. Many people see voice recognition as a 'solution' to lots of problems presented by physically disabled students where they have good verbal skills. This is not always the case. The additional cognitive load put on the student in terms of understanding the system, visual perceptual skills, problem solving and correcting text, all in addition to their course work places a burden too great for some individuals.

7.6 Software

Since Windows 95, Microsoft operating systems have included the 'Accessibility Options' control panel providing a group of basic yet crucial functions. The most commonly used of these include modification for keyboard users who only use one finger and a means of preventing unwanted, additional keystrokes; there is a module to enable mouse control via the numeric keypad and the provision for controlling the PC from many external devices including some communication aids.

Most operating systems allow modification of display features such as the thickness of window borders, screen colours, icon sizes, font faces and size, etc. People with visual impairment often have these settings modified to suit their preference. Default font and size within the user's favourite word processor is also important.

Delivery of these basic settings is difficult where students move from workstation to workstation. The use of roving profiles is a good solution,

although it requires implementation by the host institution's computer services department; unfortunately this method can create problems with some networked software.

There are many software programs available in each of the categories mentioned below, addressing a variety of problems in subtly different ways. Each is recommended to capitalise on these differences in order to focus specifically on individual concerns. A number of these programs ordinarily associated with other forms of disability such as visual problems and dyslexia are often used by students with physical disabilities to assist with cognitive and literacy difficulties while generally making work easier for the student.

7.6.1 Screen Magnifiers
Some students may find it difficult to isolate items amongst a cluttered screen, such as a toolbar button. The use of software to give a small magnified image of what the cursor is over can help enormously.

7.6.2 Speech Output
Many students who input very slowly or have literacy difficulties find it helpful to use software that speaks what is input. These programs usually have the facility to speak each letter, every word and then read the entire sentence.

7.6.3 Screen Readers
Screen readers are often used by those who find reading a problem, whether due to visual scanning difficulties or a low literacy level. Some of these programs highlight each word as it is spoken, as an aid to tracking and for some reinforcing sight recognition for their reading.

7.6.4 Word prediction
With word prediction the user inputs a letter and the program tries to guess the word to be typed, if the word is shown the user selects it with a single input; if not they type the next character thus narrowing down the list of possible words. This process continues until the word is listed or the word is completed and it is added to the programs dictionary. Most word prediction systems learn the frequency of word usage, thus offering words sooner and in turn speeding up input.

This type of program is used to speed up those with very slow input, yet as most users are not touch typists it means they have to look from keyboard to screen after almost every letter. Therefore it is only useful in this way for the very slow. Alternatively it can help students with poor spelling, but here again there is a proviso. The individual must have reasonably good reading skills to differentiate the desired word from a list that appear very similar. Audible feedback can help here, but no method is foolproof.

7.6.5 Keyboard Emulators

Software that places a virtual keyboard on the screen, sitting on top of other applications, provides the full range of keys that a standard keyboard user sees and in some cases mouse control too. The better programs offer different key layouts, which can improve the efficiency of input by saving time and effort. For text input the inclusion of word prediction is crucial to speed.

7.7 Conclusion

If institutions design services and room space to suit disabled people in general, they will by default be serving their able bodied students well and reduce the additional cost of specific modifications when they arise.

Where staff work closely with individual students, familiarisation of technologies is crucial and suitable training on specific equipment for teaching and support staff will ensure that systems are reliable and the staff appreciate how the student has to work. It also assists staff to present work in an appropriate manner.

The range of equipment available for physically disabled students is so vast that assessment should be carried out by an experienced practitioner who has knowledge of the technologies and available products, and a good understanding of disability. Without this, poor recommendations could, at best, frustrate the user quelling any enthusiasm; at worst they could have a detrimental effect reducing ability and possibly causing pain and discomfort.

It is worth noting that, although these technologies, can for many, enable independent access to the curriculum, the greater the complexity of the solution the more we ask of the user. The brain power involved in deciphering all the information presented on a computer screen, extracting what is pertinent and using it to best advantage, is often taken for granted – add to this the normal workload of studying and meeting deadlines. Only then can we begin to understand the huge cognitive burden placed on the student. Finally it must be stressed that there are many technologies not mentioned in this chapter, e.g.

page turners, desk extensions, environmental control, integrated systems, controlling the computer via brain waves, to mention a few. They have been omitted to preserve the balance and therefore this should not be read as a definitive guide.

7.8 References

[1]   www.becta.org.uk/technology/
      infosheets

E-learning: accessible, usable learning materials for all students

4

Preface

Lawrie Phipps and **Allan Sutherland**

One of the frequently espoused virtues of e-learning is the flexibility it can provide for both learners and institutions. But if the online experience for disabled students can be up to 6 times more difficult [1] then how flexible is that? Many of these difficulties can be minimised by the application of accessible and universal design of Web-based content.

Further education

In further education, a great deal has been achieved since the publication of the 1996 Tomlinson Report [1], which identified the need for a more inclusive further education sector. One of the tangible outcomes of the Tomlinson Report was the production and implementation of Inclusive Learning Action Plans (ILAPs), which were the result of deliberation, planning and commitment across colleges – often including governors, principals and specialists in the process. A typical ILAP is likely to contain references to issues such as learning styles, learner support, staff training and institutional auditing mechanisms.

The Higginson Report was published in 1996 [2] and stressed the importance of Information Learning Technologies (ILT) in further education. Many of its recommendations have been implemented through the work of the FEILT committee and now through the National Learning Network. Initiatives have included the QUILT programme, ILT strategies and ILT champions in every college. As with ILAPs, ILT strategies have become important documents in colleges, pulling together issues such as IT infrastructure, staff development and materials. There has frequently been a high level of institutional commitment to ILT strategies, including governors, principals and specialists.

Given all of this strategic commitment to inclusive learning and ILT in recent years, key questions for many colleges are:

- what does our ILT strategy have to say about inclusive learning?
- what does our Inclusive Learning Action Plan say about ILT?
- what level of awareness do our ILT champions have about the needs of disabled students and students with learning difficulties?
- how much do our inclusive learning teams know about accessible and assistive technologies?

During the last year TechDis has undertaken a series of regional and national briefings covering more than 60% of colleges. When questions such as these have been asked of college staff at these workshops, the answers have consistently been 'not very much'. It is the view of TechDis and others working in this field that it is of increasingly urgent importance that these answers should change to something like 'a great deal'.

The lessons that FE learned from Tomlinson and Higginson have been important and hard-won. One of the most important has been that without strategic commitment to developments such as Inclusive Learning and ILT then it is extremely difficult to make the kind of institutional and cultural change that is needed. Indeed, it was likened to 'chasing shadows' by one delegate at a TechDis briefing. Similarly, without staff development and training (such as that provided for ILT champions and IT co-ordinators) to accompany this strategic change then progress becomes even more difficult to achieve. Without staff awareness and skills, the potentiality of implementing strategies is severely reduced.

Higher education

Higher education has been very proactive in meeting the needs of a diverse student population and many systems are in place that allow flexibility and adaptation in the curriculum. Some of these good practices can be found in the recently published 'Accessible Curricula: Good Practice For All' [3]. This and other initiatives such as the National Disability Team and the associated projects [4] are building capacity in higher education to meet the needs of disabled students across a wide range of learning and teaching activity.

However, there is still much work to be done in the field of learning technology. The proliferation of electronic material, virtual field courses, virtual learning environments and computer aided assessment will need specific attention if they are to be made available to as wide a range of students as possible. All staff involved in learning technology, be they working full time as a learning technologist or a lecturer who sometimes saves their work as HTML, must understand the basic issues that these types of materials will raise for disabled students. Furthermore, it needs to be the role of learning technologists, not only to address the issues of making material accessible, but also to find new and innovative ways of using technology to support disabled students.

Strategies for developing and using accessible electronic materials need to be embedded in institutional learning and teaching strategies. Reference should also be made to institutional disability statements and where possible learning technologists should have meetings with disability support officers and have an open discussion about what learning technologies are and what the needs of disabled students are. Only when there is a dialogue can real progress be made.

This section provides important information and practice that will enable FE and HE institutions to approach the challenges of accessible technology in strategic ways that can include all staff and students.

[1] FEFC (1996), Inclusive Learning (the Tomlinson Report), Coventry, FEFC/HMSO

[2] FEFC (1996) Report of the Learning and Technology Committee (the Higginson Report), Coventry, FEFC,

[3] Doyle, C. and Robson, K. (2002), Accessible Curricula: Good Practice for All, Cardiff, University of Wales Institute, available from: **www.techdis.ac.uk/pdf/curricula.pdf**

[4] **www.natdisteam.ac.uk/projects.html**

Creating accessible e-learning content

Chapter 8

David Sloan, Digital Media Access Group

8.1 Introduction

E-learning providers have the moral and legislative responsibilities to ensure that users with disabilities do not encounter unjustified discrimination. It is vital to ensure that online educational resources are accessible to the widest possible audience. The benefits of accessible design include resources that can be used by a wide range of users in a diverse range of browsing environments. To help capitalise on the potential of the Web as a powerful platform for innovation in teaching and learning and to grasp the opportunity to widen access to education, this chapter provides an overview of several tools and techniques for providing accessible Web-based e-learning.

8.2 Common accessibility problems and solutions

This section outlines some of the more common accessibility problems that may exist in a Web site, and how to overcome them. It is beyond the scope of this chapter to provide a comprehensive guide to all accessibility problems and solutions; for more details, readers are referred to the W3C Web Accessibility Initiative's Web page [1] and the many excellent Web-based resources on accessible design.

8.2.1 Page and site mark-up: accessibility problems

A significant problem with many Web resources is that they are written in non-valid HTML, particularly those created semi-automatically with software such as Web authoring tools and courseware. Web pages written in non-valid HTML can struggle to interpret proprietary code written for specific browsers. The inappropriate use of HTML elements may actually cause assistive technologies for disabled Web users to interpret and present information inaccurately, limiting browsing efficiency. For example, some screen readers have the ability to allow navigation through headings and sub-headings of a Web document, but if appropriate HTML elements are not used to define headings, this functionality is lost.

Other HTML features such as tables and forms can also confuse some Web browsers. If coded inappropriately, they can cause non-visual browsers, which may read tables in a linear fashion, to lose important data structure and relationships. Some screen readers allow enhanced navigation within data tables, but again, this relies on appropriate mark-up of table structure.

Careless use of HTML tables to provide a columnar page layout can result in a confusing presentation of information in non-graphic browsers, where the effect might be of reading from left to right the first line of each column of a newspaper, then the second line of each column, and so on. An excellent demonstration of how such problems can arise is provided in the tutorial of the WAVE accessibility checking tool [2].

8.2.2 Page and site mark-up: accessibility solutions

Web content should be written in valid HTML, following specifications set by the World Wide Web Consortium (W3C) [3]. Web pages should include in the HTML code a declaration statement of the version of HTML being used, as well as a statement of the natural language of the document. Using a validation tool such as the W3C HTML Validator helps to ensure that code is valid. HTML elements should be used to reflect page structure by marking-up key structural elements such as headings and lists. Special attention should also be paid to marking-up tables and forms.

HTML elements have been provided to allow better rendering of tables and forms in linear or non-graphic environments. HTML elements exist to allow detailed structural mark-up of data tables, including row and column headers, mark-up indicating sub-headings, and groups of columns and rows. For some very complex tables, however, it may be necessary to provide a separate textual description of the contained data.

Similarly, for forms, elements and attributes to provide assistive technologies with more information about form structure should also be used. All necessary components of a Web form should appear in a logical progression to people who cannot see the form. The instructions should appear first, followed by input fields with associated labels, with a 'submit' button as the last feature of the form.

When considering page layout, CSS is the preferred technology for specifying layout and appearance. However, due to current limitations of support for CSS, tables can sometimes be the only realistic means of providing a specific layout. In such cases, care should be taken to ensure that the information on the page still makes sense when viewed in a linear browser such as Lynx, or heard through a text-to-speech browsing set-up. Tables used for layout purposes should be clearly identified using the summary attribute.

While Adobe's Portable Document Format (PDF) is a useful format for providing documents on the Web, which preserves appearance regardless of platform, PDF access through a screen reader is unpredictable. Despite recent advances made by Adobe in the area of accessible PDF creation, accessibility to blind and visually-impaired users cannot currently be guaranteed. Therefore this file format should not be relied upon as the only way of providing information and should not be used as a replacement for HTML. The most appropriate use of PDF is for downloading documents intended for printing [4].

8.2.3 Navigation: accessibility problems
Blind and visually-impaired users browsing with text-to-speech devices receive the information on a Web page in a linear fashion, i.e. line by line. Similarly, non-graphical or text-only browsers present information in a linear format. This can drastically increase browsing time. To address this issue, users tab through links on a page, listening to each hyperlink in order to gain an idea of the page content and where they can go from that page. Therefore poorly placed and labeled navigational features, which may be a nuisance to sighted users, might actually hinder accessibility for blind and visually-impaired users.

Many visually and physically disabled Web users cannot use a mouse, and are forced to rely on the keyboard or some other device to navigate the site and to input information. Additionally, some browsing set-ups may not have a mouse, such as television-based browsing environments or mobile Internet devices. Unfortunately, many Web sites implement features that require mouse action in

order to access information that is not accessible via the keyboard.

8.2.4 Navigation: accessibility solutions
The text of hyperlinks should clearly indicate the destination page. A poor example of hyperlink text (link text underlined) might be:
<u>Click here</u> to find out about the mating habits of dolphins.

A good example of hyperlink text (link text underlined) might be:
<u>Dolphins and their mating habits</u>

Pages in a Web site should always have appropriate titles and where possible, hyperlink text should be consistent with titles and headings on the destination page. To supplement navigation, a well-designed, easy-to-use and accurate search facility can help to locate information quickly. Similarly, a site map, listing all pages, can provide an accessible way for users to navigate to specific information.

To avoid confusion, links should not open destination pages in separate browser windows without explicitly informing users that this will happen, and links to non-HTML documents should also be clearly indicated.

Client-side JavaScript should not be relied upon as a means of providing navigational features – links activated by JavaScript may mean information becomes inaccessible when JavaScript is turned off or not supported.

Any information accessible via a mouse action must also be accessible via the keyboard. You can enhance keyboard navigation and control by ensuring that forms can be followed logically via the keyboard and that keyboard shortcuts are provided to access important content.

Until browser support for Cascading Style Sheets can be used to specify page layout for a specific browsing devices, a useful interim technique is to provide internal page links to important content. This allows more efficient navigation, which particularly benefits users of auditory and other non-graphic browsing environments [5].

8.2.5 Page appearance: accessibility problems
Text marked up in HTML is in theory accessible to the majority of current Web users, although the use of multimedia enhances accessibility for those with low levels of literacy, learning disabilities and other

cognitive impairments [6]. Variables in the appearance of text can affect accessibility, including font size, style, colour, and background colour. Several conditions can affect a text's readability, including many variations of colour-blindness and dyslexia.

If colour alone is used to distinguish information, these users may encounter difficulty in accessing the material. Low contrast between text and background colours, and certain colour combinations may cause problems in reading the material. Red/green colour schemes are particularly troublesome for many colour-blind people, while red/blue text and background schemes cause chromostereopsis, an unpleasant temporary visual condition [7].

Spelling and grammatical errors tend to be accentuated when heard through a text-to-speech device; acronyms and text in a foreign language may also cause these devices difficulty.

The use of frames in page design can cause accessibility and usability problems for users of some assistive technologies and non-graphical browsers, and can also confuse non-human agents such as search engine robots.

8.2.6 Page appearance: accessibility solutions

Clear language and correct spelling and grammar increases the accessibility of text on a Web page. Wherever possible, text should be broken into lists or short paragraphs. Avoid using a variety of different text appearance option. Instead, choose a sensible default text that can be changed by users. Text font size should be specified in relative terms, allowing users to alter it to suit their eyesight and/or screen resolution.
Creating a good contrast between default text and background colours is vital. Colour should not be relied on solely to distinguish information since this will potentially confuse blind or visually-impaired users.

The recommended way of controlling page appearance is through use of Cascading Style Sheets (CSS). Here, characteristics which govern the appearance of the text are stored separately to the Web page content, and can be changed by users if necessary, through user-defined style sheets. With a combination of appropriately marked-up text and the judicious use of CSS, it is possible to create attractive Web pages that can be adjusted to suit an individual user's specific requirements. Given current variation in browser support for CSS, Web pages should be tested

using CSS in a variety of browsers. It is necessary to ensure that information is still accessible when CSS are not supported at all.

If frames are used in Web pages, ensure that users can access the content with browsers that do not support frames. Each frame should be given a meaningful title indicating the frame's content and the <noframe> element should be used to present information explaining page layout and frame content.

8.3 Graphic and multi-media content – accessibility issues

Graphics and multimedia can add tremendous value to Web content, particularly in augmenting textual information. Complex concepts or objects that may be difficult to describe in text form can be more effectively represented through use of multimedia. Using multimedia to show dynamic changes to an object over time can also enhance learning. Multimedia also allows users interactivity, since it can respond to user input.

There are, however, many potential accessibility problems associated with multimedia Web content. For example, blind and visually-impaired users who use auditory browsing devices may be unable to access visual content; similarly, this content will be inaccessible to users of other non-graphic browsing environments. Deaf or hard-of-hearing users may be unable to access audio content. Since some interactive content requires fine control through the use of a mouse, students with mobility impairments who may be using alternative input devices may find it difficult to make these fine adjustments. Users with certain cognitive disabilities may be confused by rapidly changing content and flashing content may trigger photo-sensitive epilepsy.

The sheer variety of formats in multimedia content can also cause access problems. While graphical browsers can normally display static image files without difficulty, formats of animated or audiovisual content often require a proprietary media player. Browser support for multimedia content can therefore be unreliable.

The demands that multimedia content places on bandwidth may also affect accessibility. Web users with low bandwidth Internet connections may experience severe difficulty accessing multimedia resources.

8.3.1 Accessibility solutions for graphic and multi-media content

The core principle in designing graphics and multimedia for accessibility is to ensure as far as possible that information provided by graphical and multimedia content is also provided in an accessible format. This is preferable to removing altogether multimedia content that may be inaccessible to some users.

For simple graphics, HTML provides an attribute for the <img> element, the <alt> attribute, often referred to as 'ALT Text'. Including an <alt> command will provide a text description of an image for individuals using non-graphic browsers. It is not enough simply to describe the graphic in generic terms. 'ALT text' should provide the same information as the graphic, which is **not necessarily** the same as a description of the graphic.

Some other points to consider when supplying the text-alternatives to images and graphics:

▶ for complex graphics that provide complex information, such as graphs or charts, a separate text description should be provided. While the longdesc attribute of the <img> element can be used to specify a file containing the textual description, it is not widely supported. Creating a prominent link near the image to the textual description of the information provided by the image is a good alternative.
▶ for graphics that serve as navigational links, alternative text should indicate the destination of the link.
▶ for image maps, alternative text must be supplied for the main image as well as each hotspot. Since some browsing technologies may not support image maps, a redundant set of textual hyperlinks should be provided elsewhere on the page,
▶ graphics containing text should be avoided where possible, as the appearance of the text cannot be changed. If they are used, the alternative text should contain identical text to the graphic,
▶ graphics which provide no information to users, usually graphics which are used to control the layout of a page, should have null alternative text, i.e. alt="", explicitly indicating that the image has no content value.

Providing accessible audio or visual content presents significantly more challenges than providing accessible static graphics. Captions are required for the spoken word, plus any other audio output, and textual descriptions are required for all visual content. These textual alternatives can become very complex, particularly where time-dependent information is provided by dynamic content such as video or animated material.

It is possible to embed captions within the multimedia object through captioning tools such as Magpie [8]. Where possible, such techniques should be explored. Often, however, a compromise may have to be made, for example by providing captions as an alternative to audio content, and a separate textual transcription of the multimedia clip.

Content provided through the use of client-side JavaScript should be accessible in other forms when scripts are turned off or not supported. In many cases client-side JavaScript is used for visual display effects such as image swapping, and as long as such effects do not provide information to users, they should not present potential accessibility problems.

Macromedia's Flash, a proprietary file format widely used for providing dynamic audio-visual content, can greatly enhance the browsing experience. However Flash can also result in content that is inaccessible to many users, including those with a visual or motor impairment.

In February 2002, Macromedia introduced the Flash MX authoring environment and the Flash 6 player. This combination introduced enhanced accessibility features, including the potential for some Flash content to be made accessible to certain screen readers. Wherever possible these accessibility features should be used when creating and viewing Flash content.

Java-based Web applications (applets) are another way of providing interactive multimedia content that can greatly enhance teaching and learning resources. To help to reduce potential accessibility problems, IBM's Java Accessibility Checklist [9] provides Java developers with additional guidance on creating accessible resources. Java applets should be created with the Java Accessibility API [10], which contains classes and programming language interfaces designed to allow information from graphical applications to be made available to assistive technologies.

8.4 Accessibility and authoring environments

The simplest way to create accessible Web resources is to hand-code HTML using a basic text-editor. While authors have full control over the code created, and can insert accessibility features such as alternative text for images as they go, this can be a painstaking way of creating Web content and requires advanced knowledge of HTML.

Alternatively, there are many popular authoring tools available to semi-automate the process of Web content creation. These allow authors without in-depth knowledge of HTML and other Web technologies rapidly to create resources with a professional look. Specific courseware authoring tools such as those provided by Blackboard and WebCT allow the easy creation of content geared towards learning and teaching.

Clearly, there is a huge advantage in using authoring tools to create content. In theory, such tools actually promote Web accessibility by allowing easy access to Web content contribution from individuals without expertise in Web authoring.

However, content created by authoring tools can present problems. Authoring tools frequently generate non-valid HTML, complete with proprietary tags. Often, they do not promote insertion of accessibility features such as alternative text for images. All this results all too often in inaccessible Web content. In this way, the lack of awareness of many content providers in accessible design issues is accentuated by the relative failure of popular authoring tools to promote the creation of accessible resources.

The W3Cs Authoring Tool Accessibility Guidelines (ATAG) [11] provides a checklist of features with which authoring tools should comply in order to ensure that the content they produce is as accessible as possible. At the time of writing, however, support amongst authoring tools of the ATAG is inconsistent. Fortunately, since the amendment of Section 508 of the Rehabilitation Act came into effect in the US in 2000, there has been a flurry of development of accessibility checking and retrofitting tools, and some of these are now integrated into popular authoring tools. A similar effect is noticeable in authoring tools aimed specifically at the learning technology sector, and accessibility of courseware authoring tools such as those provided by Blackboard and WebCT is now being addressed. Accessibility

checking tools are discussed in more detail in the next section.

Online accessibility resources are available for many providers of Web content authoring tools, including:

- Macromedia (Dreamweaver, Ultradev, Cold Fusion, Flash, Director) [12],
- Microsoft (FrontPage) [13],
- Adobe (GoLive, Acrobat) [14],
- Blackboard Accessibility [15],
- WebCT Accessibility [16].

Even with an authoring tool specifically designed to create fully accessible content, it is vital for content authors to be aware of accessible design techniques, particularly in light of the current constraints affecting Web development environments. Content developers should be aware of the limitations of authoring tools in creating accessible content and should ensure that all resources created are not only designed with accessibility in mind but are checked for accessibility throughout the design lifecycle of the resource.

8.5 Accessibility checking techniques

Techniques for avoiding potential accessibility problems have been discussed, but how can e-learning resource providers spot potential accessibility problems in existing resources? A methodology for assessing Web sites for accessibility is presented by Sloan et al [17]. This methodology discusses a number of checks for accessibility barriers. These include:

- utilising free accessibility checking tools, such as Bobby, A-Prompt or the TechDis Accessibility and Usability checker (see below),
- manually checking resources. Using the browser, can the text size and style be adjusted by the user? Is the site still readable when style information is removed? Can the resource be used without a mouse?
- testing in different browsing environments, including non-graphic browsers such as Lynx. This is particularly important where the resource will be used as a Web application accessible from diverse browsing environments,
- using the resource with assistive technologies such as screen readers, speech browsers or screen magnifiers. Tools such as Vischeck [18] provide simulations of certain visual

impairments and can also provide useful feedback,

▶ evaluating the resource with disabled people. While the above checks may help to identify most accessibility problems, some issues will only become apparent when observing a disabled person use the resource.

8.6 Free accessibility checking tools

There are a number of useful free accessibility checking tools available as Web services or which can be downloaded. A fuller list of tools is provided by the W3C Web Accessibility Initiative [1]. Some of the most useful tools are listed below:

Bobby: The original and probably best-known Web accessibility-checking tool is free and allows one page to be checked at a time. A version of this software which checks a whole site in one go could in the past be downloaded free of charge but now costs $99 for a single user copy [19].

A-Prompt: An excellent alternative available from the Adaptive Technology Research Project at the University of Toronto. A-Prompt can be downloaded free of charge. It not only identifies access problems but also allows limited repairs [20].

The WAVE: Another useful free Web-based accessibility checker, adding text and icons to a page to alert the developer to potential accessibility problems. It is supplied with highly informative documentation and gives examples of poor design [21].

Page Valet and Site Valet: Free, Web-based validation tool, which concentrates on validation of HTML code but includes an optional accessibility checker [22].

W3C HTML Validator: Not an accessibility checker as such but since many accessibility problems stem from invalid HTML, this is a vital component in checking for accessibility. The W3C HTML Validation service offers validation of individual pages against various specifications of HTML and includes a validator for Cascading Style Sheets (CSS) [23].

HTML Tidy: Again, this not specifically an accessibility checker. It identifies and repairs invalid HTML and can be downloaded free of charge [24].

TechDis Accessibility and Usability Validator: Presents seven precepts of usable and accessible design against which pages can be checked. A semi-automatic tool is available on registration [25].

8.7 Accessibility software

Comprehensive accessibility and usability checking tools are increasingly available, sometimes bundled with popular authoring tools. Some of these incorporate 'accessibility retrofitting' functionality, where HTML code is repaired automatically. These packages include:

InFocus: Accessibility checking and retrofitting software by SSB Technologies. SSB Technologies also offer the free 'Ask Alice' Accessibility checking service. Insight LE is available as a free plug-in for the Adobe GoLive Web authoring tools [26].

AccVerify, AccRepair and AccMonitor from HiSoftware: AccVerify SE is available as a free plug-in free for users of Microsoft FrontPage [27].

Lift Accessibility and Usability Checker from UsableNet: Lift is available as an online subscription service and as a version for Macromedia Dreamweaver and UltraDev [28].

It appears that the implementation of (the anti-discrimination) Section 508 legislation in the US has been largely responsible for the increased demand for and recent proliferation of these accessibility tools. As a result, the documentation and functionality of the tools is frequently geared towards US customers and the goal of compliance with Section 508. International users may therefore find it difficult to achieve compliance with WAI guidelines using these tools.

It is also important to remember that even with the software listed above, manual intervention will always be required to ensure that accessibility problems do not remain. Additionally, while a resource may be technically validated as accessible, there may still be significant problems with its use. So purchasing a very expensive accessibility checking tool cannot on its own ensure optimal usability and accessibility.

8.8 Conclusion

There are many techniques for designing Web content that does not contain accessibility barriers. Even where barriers cannot be avoided, the use of equivalent alternatives will ensure that as many students as possible can use e-learning resources. Implementing accessible design techniques should never result in a diminished resource. Instead, accessible design frequently achieves a more usable and portable solution for the widest range of individuals and browsing environments. While authoring tools and automatic checking tools can make it much easier to create accessible content, it is crucial for content developers to be aware of accessibility issues and how they can be avoided.

8.9 References

[1]   W3C Web Accessibility Initiative: **www.w3.org/WAI**

[2]   Examples of table accessibility, provided by a tutorial for the WAVE accessibility assessment tool, available from: **www.temple.edu/inst_disabilities/piat/ wave/doc/index.html**

[3]   W3C HTML specifications, available from: **www.w3.org/TR**

[4]   Nielsen, J. (2001), Avoid PDF for On-screen Reading, available from: **www.useit.com/ alertbox/20010610.html**

[5]   Implementing Skip Navigation, available from: **www.dmag.org.uk/resources/ design_articles/skip.asp**

[6]   Jiwnani, K. (2001), Design for Users with Cognitive Disabilities, available from: **www.otal.umd.edu/UUPractice/ cognition**

[7]   Pearrow, M. (2000), **Web Usability Handbook.** Charles River Media, Inc.

[8]   Media Access Generator (Magpie), available from: **http://ncam.wgbh.org/ Webaccess/magpie/index.html**

[9]   IBM Java Accessibility Guidelines, available from: **www-3.ibm.com/able/accessjava.html**

[10] Java Accessibility API: **http://java.sun.com/ products/jfc/jaccess-1.2.2/doc**

[11] W3C Authoring Tool Accessibility Guidelines, available from: **www.w3.org/TR/ATAG10**

[12] **www.macromedia.com/macromedia/ accessibility**

[13] **www.microsoft.com/enable**

[14] **http://access.adobe.com**

[15] **http://products.blackboard.com/ cp/bb5/access/index.cgi**

[16] **http://www.Webct.com/products/ viewpage?name=products_accessibility**

[17] Sloan, D., Rowan, M., Gregor, P. and Booth, P. (2000), Accessible Accessibility. In Scholtz, J and Thomas, J. (Eds), Proceedings of Conference on Universal Usability (CUU 2000). Association for Computing Machinery, Inc. (ACM) 96-101.

[18] Vischeck Colourblindness simulator: **http://vischeck.com**

[19] **http://cast.org/bobby**

[20] **http://aprompt.snow.utoronto.ca**

[21] **www.temple.edu/inst_disabilities/piat/ wave**

[22] **http://valet.webthing.com**

[23] **http://validator.w3.org**

[24] **www.w3.org/People/Raggett/tidy** and **http://tidy.sourceforge.net**

[25] **www.techdis.ac.uk**

[26] **http://www.ssbtechnologies.com**

[27] **http://www.hisoftware.com**

[28] **http://www.usablenet.com**

Chapter 9

Achieving SENDA-compliance for Web sites in further and higher education: an art or a science?

NAJ Witt and **AP McDermott,** University of Plymouth

9.1 Introduction

In recent months the further and higher education community has become increasingly aware of the issues surrounding the Special Educational Needs and Disability Act (2001) (SENDA). The main emphasis has been on the impact of the Act on the development of Managed Learning Environments and Virtual Learning Environments (VLEs).

Institutions must not only address accessibility issues related to these environments but also apply the same rigour and good practice to all Web sites (extranet and intranet) that form part of an institution's communication strategy. Complying with the Act is now a high priority for many institutions, thanks to the efforts of groups such as TechDis [1], Royal National Institute for the Blind [2] and Institute for Learning and Teaching [3] in raising awareness of SENDA for the delivery of online education and training. Institutions need to take a comprehensive approach to the issue of accessibility to ensure that this awareness is put into practice and that in turn, this practice forms part of the provision of all electronic services.

Browning and Lowndes [4] found that many education institutions are struggling to maintain their Web sites. Further and higher education institutions experienced problems in: a lack of authority control over the design, navigation and content of faculty Web sites, the presence of out of date material, and the constriction of the Webmaster bottleneck. Many institutions have taken to employing individuals especially to coordinate departmental sites thereby regaining the authority control and applying uniformity to design, navigation and content.

One way of dealing with this struggle is to implement a co-ordinated approach with central support, tight content management and strict design standards. This may be supplemented by the use of design templates and content management systems. This corporate approach has met with some resistance within the education sector probably as a result of the way that such sites have evolved. An audit by the authors revealed that most institutions have a corporate site linked to faculty, department, division or group sub-sites. While elements of consistency exist between different parts of most sub-sites, there is an obvious mark of ownership in sub-sites with their own layout, design and structure. Through their individual identities, these sites may cause concern to an institution trying to ensure that all its Web sites meet the accessibility criteria.

In this chapter we will outline the various guidelines and standards that exist, explore approaches to meeting these and give a case study to illustrate the issues and skills involved.

9.2 Guidelines, standards or legislation?

Web site developers should be aware of the World Wide Web Consortium (W3C) which develops interoperable technologies (specifications, guidelines, software, and tools) to 'lead the Web to its full potential as a forum for information, commerce, communication, and collective understanding' [5]. An important W3C programme is the Web Accessibility Initiative (WAI), which attempts to increase accessibility to the Web through five complementary strategies:

- ensuring that Web technologies support accessibility,
- developing guidelines for accessibility,
- developing tools to evaluate and facilitate accessibility,
- conducting education and outreach,
- co-ordinating Web design with research and development [6].

Organisations in the further and higher education sectors should look to the WAI for the provision of accessibility guidelines. In addition to the WAI, W3C has researched and developed extensive guidelines for the use of Web technologies such as HTML, XML and CSS, and these should be used to generate products that are not only useful to disabled students, but also interoperable across a number of platforms.

W3C have produced a list of Checkpoints for Web Content Accessibility Guidelines (WCAG) 1.0. This is a hierarchical structure consisting of three priority levels:

- **Priority 1 (Level A):** This is the minimum level of accessibility that Web content developers should be working towards. While this removes some barriers to accessing Web material, many disabled students would still be excluded from using it.
- **Priority 2 (Level AA):** Achieving this level will remove more barriers to accessibility although some students will still be excluded from using the Web material.
- **Priority 3 (Level AAA):** Satisfying the Priority 3 criteria will provide access to Web material for most disabled users.

Adherence to the WAI guidelines does not guarantee accessibility for every individual. Developers need to think in terms of 'inclusive design' or of applying the guidelines so that design does not automatically exclude any group of individuals. This principle should guide both the environment and content development stages. Thus, both developers and information providers must be aware of accessibility issues. Table 1 shows a summary of the checkpoints for Web content accessibility guidelines.

9.3 Can we learn any lessons from the US?

As outlined in Chapter 3, the agencies of the European Union are moving towards legislation on the subject of increasing accessibility to facilities. This process follows the introduction in the US of Section 508 [7].

In the US, the Acquisition of Electronic and Information Technology under Section 508 of the Rehabilitation Act requires federal agencies to ensure that their electronic and information technology is accessible to disabled individuals. Section 508 applies to both intranet and Internet

information and applications and includes:

- software applications and operating systems,
- telecommunication products,
- video and multimedia products,
- self-contained, closed products,
- desktop and portable computers.

Section 508 uses the US federal procurement process to ensure that technology acquired by the federal government is accessible. A set of standards rather than guidelines is in use, which includes standards for software and Web-based information and applications.

There are notable differences between Section 508 and WCAG Level A (Priority 1). If a Web site complies with Level-A (Priority 1) and the developer also wants it to comply with Section 508, these are the five additional standards of Section 508 that must be addressed:

- when pages utilise scripting languages to display content, or to create interface elements, the information provided by the script must be identified with functional text that can be read by assistive technology,
- when a Web page requires that an applet, plug-in or other application be present on the client system to interpret page content, the page must provide a link to a plug-in or applet,
- when electronic forms are designed to be completed online, the form must allow individuals using assistive technology to access the information, field elements and functionality required for completion and submission of the form, including all directions and cues,
- a method must be provided which permits users to bypass repetitive navigation links,
- a user must be alerted when a timed response is required and given sufficient time to indicate that more time is required.

If a Web site complies with Section 508 and its developer wishes it to comply also with WCAG Level A (Priority 1), there are four additional checkpoints that must be addressed:

- until software is developed which can automatically read aloud the text equivalent of a visual track, provide an auditory description of the important information of the visual track of a multimedia presentation,
- clearly identify changes in the natural language of a document's text and any text equivalents (e.g., captions),
- ensure that equivalents for dynamic content

are updated when the dynamic content changes,

▶ use the clearest and simplest language appropriate for a site's content.

9.4 How to achieve compliance

Further and higher education institutions should regard WCAG Level A (Priority 1) as the starting point for the development of their Web site. For an inclusive Web site, you should investigate and attempt to adopt fully the guidelines for Level AA (Priority 2) and Level AAA (Priority 3).

In the US, Section 508 has put accessibility high on the agenda for software developers, with companies such as Macromedia, Adobe and Microsoft all prioritising accessibility issues. UK institutions can therefore benefit from this initiative by using the accessibility tools in off-the-shelf software to assist in the creation of a Section 508-compliant Web site.

Macromedia, the developers of Dreamweaver and Flash, have released their Solutions Kit: Accessibility and E-Learning [8]. This provides software extensions for diagnosing and retrofitting a Web site for accessibility as well as training courses, white papers and case studies. The Royal National Institute of the Blind (RNIB) have established a dialogue with Macromedia and report that the kit assists developers by providing guidelines and software features for assessing Web sites for accessibility, and by providing guidance for creating or retrofitting sites based on Section 508 requirements. This cannot in itself ensure an accessible site; the only way to ensure that a Web site is accessible is through deliberate development, testing and evaluation informed by human judgement [9].

Adobe have included accessibility features in Acrobat 5 which allow users to create accessible Adobe PDF documents [10]. Another Adobe product, GoLive, can help users to create accessible Web sites and allows the installation of a plug-in that automatically identifies Section 508 violations in Web pages created with GoLive [11]. Similar functionality can be added to Macromedia Dreamweaver with the addition of the LIFT plug-in [12].

9.5 Strict HTML as the way forward?

Since 1998, W3C has corrected errors, including minor typographical errors, in the specification of HTML 4.0 resulting in the version HTML 4.01. This version allows Web developers to create style sheets that permit increased control over the visual presentation of a document such as typeface, font colour, alignment and layout.

HTML 4.01 further enhances functionality compared to version 4.0, namely through:

▶ internationalisation,
▶ accessibility,
▶ enhanced tables,
▶ embedding objects,
▶ enhanced scripting.

Style sheets are intended to replace many tags previously used for controlling presentation and such tags have been designated as 'deprecated' by HTML 4.01. Deprecated tags may be used at present but will become obsolete as style sheets give developers greater control over presentation.

Other features that support accessibility in HTML 4.01 include the ability to mark-up the description of an object, the requirement of alternate text for images, support for the abbreviation and acronym elements, and longer descriptions for tables, frames, and images.

HTML 4.01 allows greater control over layout and structure. The inclusion of tabular information such as column widths allows tables to display data incrementally as it arrives, rather than waiting to receive the entire table before displaying it. It is also easier to embed objects such as images, video, sound, or other specialised applications.

HTML 4.01 is available on three different levels and developers can choose the more applicable option. Each level adheres to a varying degree to the HTML 4.01 specification:

▶ **HTML 4.01 Strict Document Type Definition (DTD).** This definition adheres more closely to the specification than the others. It uses no deprecated tags, opting instead for the use of style sheets, and does not use frames.
▶ **HTML 4.01 Transitional DTD.** This definition includes all deprecated tags, but does not include frames.

44

◗ **HTML 4.01 Frameset DTD.** This definition includes all deprecated tags and also includes frames.

HTML 4.01 Strict DTD gives Web developers a rigid protocol, which, if adhered to, allows them to produce a Web site that will comply with WCAG Levels A, AA, and AAA (Priorities 1, 2 and 3). The use of Transitional or Frameset DTD makes it virtually impossible to achieve Levels AA or AAA (Priorities 2 or 3).

9.6 Tools to aid compliance

Many tools can be used to support Web page development including:

◗ **Evaluation tools:** These perform a static analysis of pages or sites regarding their accessibility and return a report or a rating.
◗ **Repair tools:** These can identify problems with a Web page or site and recommend improvements to increase accessibility.
◗ **Filter and transformation tools:** These tools assist Web users rather than developers and either modify a page or supplement an assistive technology or browser.

A recent preliminary audit of accessibility software has identified more than 30 site-evaluation tools, 10 Web page repair tools and over 20 filter and transformation tools. At least some of these may facilitate the production of a set of Web pages compliant with W3C WAI and/or the USA Section 508. Likewise, some may generate output that enables online material to meet the requirements of SENDA.

One of the most used tools is Bobby. This has been developed by the Center for Applied Special Technology (CAST), which worked closely with the W3C to create an evaluation tool employing their Web Content Accessibility Guidelines and providing page and site evaluation support for developers. The latest version, Bobby WorldWide, available from CAST's Web site [13] supports analysis of Web pages for compliance with Section 508, Level A (Priority 1), Level AA (Priority 2) and Level AAA (Priority 3) guidelines.

Developers can submit a Web page address to Bobby to obtain an online accessibility report though this provides a report for a single page only. For a report covering a number of pages, you can purchase a fuller version of Bobby that allows the batch processing of groups of Web pages or

Guideline 1. Provide equivalent alternatives to auditory and visual content
Provide content that conveys to the user essentially the same function or purpose as auditory or visual content.

Guideline 2. Don't rely on colour alone
Ensure that text and graphics are easily understood when viewed without colour.

Guideline 3. Use mark-up and style sheets and do so properly
Mark-up documents with the proper structural elements. Control presentation with style sheets rather than with presentation elements and attributes.

Guideline 4. Clarify natural language usage
Use mark-up that facilitates pronunciation or interpretation of abbreviated or foreign text.

Guideline 5. Create tables that transform gracefully
Ensure that tables have the necessary mark-up to allow a user's browser to display them correctly.

Guideline 6. Ensure that pages featuring new technologies transform gracefully
Ensure that pages are accessible even when newer technologies are not supported or are turned off.

Guideline 7. Ensure user control of time-sensitive content changes
Ensure that users can pause or stop moving, blinking, scrolling, or auto-updating objects or pages.

Guideline 8. Ensure direct accessibility of embedded user interfaces
Ensure that the user-interface follows principles of accessible design: device-independent access to functionality, keyboard operability, self-voicing, etc.

Guideline 9. Design for device-independence
Use features that enable page elements to be activated regardless of input devise used.

Guideline 10. Use interim solutions
Use interim accessibility solutions so that assistive technologies and older browsers will operate correctly.

Guideline 11. Use W3C technologies and guidelines
Use W3C technologies (according to specification) and follow accessibility guidelines. Where it is not possible to use a W3C technology, or when doing so results in material that does not transform gracefully, provide an alternative version of the content that is accessible.

Guideline 12. Provide context and orientation information
Provide context and orientation information to help users understand complex pages or elements.

Guideline 13. Provide clear navigation mechanisms
Provide clear and consistent navigation mechanisms, such as orientation information, navigation bars, a site map, etc., to increase the likelihood that an individual will find the desired information in a site.

Guideline 14. Ensure that documents are clear and simple
Ensure that documents are clear, simple and easily understood.

complete sites. Using Bobby effectively is dependent upon the developer's ability to interpret the final report. Deciding what modifications are necessary to achieve the required level of compliance requires knowledge of accessibility issues and HTML.

Bobby returns three information types for each of the three priority levels:

Table 1. Summary of Web content accessibility guidelines (WCAG) 1.0

a list of automatically-detected accessibility errors,

user checks which are errors that require manual examination,

general guidelines for the user to check.

A recent addition to the growing range of accessibility tools is the LIFT plug-in for Macromedia's Dreamweaver Web design software. This evaluation and repair tool is an example of a software solution to aid developers in achieving compliance with Section 508 but also has WCAG priorities built in. LIFT features include:

the ability to create usable and accessible content,

an automatic repair process for existing pages using a Fix Wizard,

the facility to create corporate guidelines and to standardise content.

LIFT can be used to check a page and produce a report suggesting improvements to the relevant set of guidelines. In some cases the developer needs to interpret this advice to ensure compliance.

It is possible to ensure that Web pages meet the required standard using tools such as Bobby and LIFT. Each package links to relevant checkpoints and gives examples and illustrations of best practice. However the developer must undertake their own audit of the Web page and interpret the advice given by the tools in order to satisfy themselves that they have achieved compliance.

9.7 Browser technology

HTML 4.01 embeds Cascading Style Sheets (CSS) within page design. When using CSS the developer needs only to specify physical attributes such as font face, size, colour and style

once for any element in the style sheet. CSS will automatically apply the specified styles whenever that element occurs. To change the style of an element the developer edits only the CSS, rather than every element. CSS has a much wider array of attributes than HTML and gives a greater choice of page elements. A CSS validator is available from W3C [14], which will generate confirmation that the CSS reaches the required standard or provides information about problems and how to correct them.

The two main browsers, Netscape and Internet Explorer, have varying levels of compliance with CSS. This means that some browser versions only support some CSS functions. To confuse things further, some browser manufacturers have developed tags that are compatible only with their own browser software. Fortunately, the latest browser versions are much more CSS-compliant than their predecessors.

The most common browsers that do not comply with CSS are:

Microsoft Internet Explorer 4.x,

Netscape Navigator 4.x,

Opera 3.5,

any older versions of the above mentioned.

It must be accepted, however, that developers cannot design for every browser. Users of Netscape Navigator/Communicator and Microsoft Internet Explorer below version 4 will not be able to access otherwise accessible sites due to the poor support for Cascading Style Sheets. Fortunately a survey of Internet browser usage, based on 320 million users accessing the Web during March 2002, shows that 95% of users employ a browser capable of using CSS and HTML 4.01, such as Netscape 6.x and above or Internet Explorer 5.x and above [15].

9.8 Putting it all together: a case study

A range of methods and guidelines for producing accessible Web sites are available through WCAG 1.0, HTML 4.01, CSS, a choice of priority levels and a range of software tools. A survey of UK further and higher education Web sites has found that there is no consistency regarding accessibility across the sector, despite the existence of guidelines which suggest that WCAG Level A (Priority 1) is the minimum that Web developers should aim for.

Figure 1: former Science site

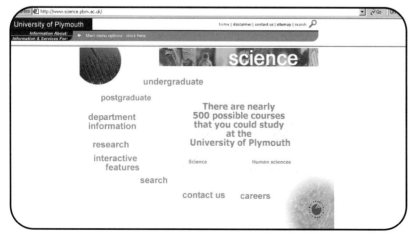

In a study that we conducted, our goal was to assess the ease of producing a WCAG-compliant Web site. It was decided to produce a Web site that complied with Level AAA (Priority 3). The starting point was the existing Faculty of Science site at the University of Plymouth, which was designed in 1999 using Macromedia Flash, together with Java and Perl. The site received critical acclaim and was awarded the distinction of Daily Telegraph Web site of the Month. It formed part of the Faculty media strategy, with complementary design elements linking paper-based and electronic media. Having undergone several minor changes in recent years, it remains a popular academic Web site with positive feedback from its users.

Recently the University has been developing a new extranet site, which has placed additional pressures on both the design and content of the Science site. This has resulted in design changes, auditing and repackaging to meet the new University direction. As an interim measure the Faculty of Science site uses frames to display the University navigation above the site's own navigation system, as seen in Figure 1.

The graphics-rich site was designed with Dreamweaver, in which design templates can be used to create new pages quickly while maintaining the original design theme. The first stage in producing an accessible design was to check the existing site with Bobby. This revealed the need for a major re-design in order to comply with accessibility standards and a decision was made that it would be easier to begin with a new design driven by accessibility rather than attempting to modify the existing site.

This approach allowed the development team to focus on the accessibility issues and the brief for the site was to:

▶ keep the design clean,
▶ keep the site simple,
▶ minimise the content,
▶ simplify navigation,
▶ use best practice.

Following an audit of available software and tools, the design teams chose to use Dreamweaver as the design tool and Bobby as a validator to check completed pages. They checked their progress with the LIFT plug-in.

The team studied the WCAG guidelines and found that while the W3C site is comprehensive,

Figure 2: new Science site

extracting the desired information can be confusing. A simplified version of the guidelines was produced to encourage discussion related to critical areas of the design. These helped the designers to focus on thematic accessibility areas from the start of the design process. Each Guideline was discussed and mapped against features in the design software.

For example, Guideline 5 requires tables to transform gracefully. To comply with this Guideline the designer must ensure that tables have the necessary HTML codes, which allow a user's browser to display them correctly. Paradoxically, the ease with which tables can be created in a package like Dreamweaver may actually be a drawback, since inserting tables within tables can cause accessibility problems. The relevant checkpoints should be investigated at the initial design stage, so that correct and meaningful annotation can be applied to tables.

Using an interactive approach, the CSS was produced and validated in conjunction with the layout design. This was then checked with LIFT running on the fly within Dreamweaver to highlight any deviation from CSS-compliance. This was further checked with Bobby. It should be noted that since both Bobby and LIFT use their own different and subjective interpretation of the guidelines, the development team had to satisfy themselves that CSS-compliance had been achieved.

This pragmatic, iterative approach soon evolved into a more rigid design methodology consisting of appraisal, planning, execution and monitoring. The appraisal stage collated the relevant guideline information and once a decision had been made as to which Priority Level would be adhered to, the applicable checkpoints were fully investigated and cross-referenced where necessary. The layout design was produced for the planning stage; this required the element descriptions, table width ratios, font attributes and the general site design to be checked for CSS-compliance.

Once the initial site design was deemed to comply with CSS, the pages could be prepared for the execution phase. Regular checks followed to ensure that the guidelines were not breached. The last stage, monitoring, revealed that accessibility requires continual assessment. If new content is added to the site or if design elements are changed, the nature of the site also changes, requiring revalidation of the site's accessibility.

The initial design produced to Priority 3 compliance is shown in Figure 2.

This process has been a steep learning curve for those involved. We have found that the WCAG priority checkpoints can be difficult to cross-reference, the validation tools require a number of subjective decisions and some of the guidance or feedback is ambiguous. The design process requires forethought and planning and the key to accessible design is to ensure that the issues become integrated in electronic media policy.

An area of concern highlighted in the audit of existing institution Web sites is the heavy reliance on validation or verification tools. Developers tend to be unaware of or overlook the high element of personal accountability in the use of these tools. For instance, while Bobby will detect a missing text description for an image, it is the developer who is responsible for annotating this image with meaningful text. Frequently, an image has a meaningless or misleading text description though the validation tool output states that the page is accessible.

9.9 Towards a UK standard

Many UK further and higher education institutions are currently debating the impact of SENDA on institutional policy. A practical set of instructions and demonstrators of best practice is needed, since compliance depends on interpretation of guidelines. There is a danger that Web accessibility may be perceived as a mechanistic or a Quality Assurance process relying on checklists and evaluation tools, which then treat accessibility as an afterthought. We need a cultural shift in education institutions, in which Web developers consider not only how their Web site will be used but also who will use it.

Priority 1 may be the choice of many institutions because it is the easiest to implement either by a re-design or retrofitting an existing site. A worrying trend in the US is the addition of a '508 and old browser' sub-site where the designers have decided to create a cut down, text-only version of their site to meet the accessibility criteria. This obviously goes against the goal for inclusiveness and it is hoped that UK education institutions will not follow this precedent.

At present, individual institutions must decide which Priority Level they wish to implement. However, it may be that a UK Web accessibility standard is required. A single standard would provide clarity for the user. A Web site designed with accessibility in mind may have the right to display a number of logos or buttons which certify that the site meets standards such as valid CSS, HTML 4.01, or that it has been verified by Bobby or can be viewed using a text browser. Users may be more reassured with a single 'accessibility achieved' type of logo rather than an array of buttons. However, if accessibility is integrated into all further and higher education Web site policies there should be no need for badges and logos as it could then be taken for granted that all education institutions' sites are accessible.

Once an institutional policy on Web accessibility has been created, it must be applied to all electronic media. With the rise of the split of information between the extranet and intranet (where the extranet is an institution's external Web site and the intranet contains information accessible only by approved users), there is a tendency to perceive accessibility as an issue relating solely to the extranet and to ignore it on the intranet. While it is a simple task to integrate accessibility into the design of an extranet by using design templates, content management systems and editorial guidelines, it can be difficult to implement the same strategy within an intranet.

Yet intranets may allow individuals to post a variety of electronic media for teaching and learning. This material is, of course, covered by SENDA and all information providers must be aware of their obligations in ensuring compliance with SENDA. This is a major challenge for education institutions.

9.10 Conclusions

UK education institutions face major challenges in complying with the terms of SENDA. Institutions without an accessibility policy that can be easily implemented will have to develop one quickly. Despite the availability of guidelines and tools there is still a degree of confusion over this issue within the further and higher education sector, with emphasis on pursuing compliance for external information. Rather than perceiving accessibility as a hurdle to jump over, institutions must develop and adopt a comprehensive approach, which includes all electronic information. As a result of the range of standards and guidelines, the levels of interpretation and the subjective judgements required in negotiating these, the creation of an accessible solution is very much an art.

9.11 References

[1]　www.techdis.ac.uk

[2]　www.rnib.org.uk

[3]　www.ilt.ac.uk

[4]　Browning, P. and Lowndes, M. (2001), JISC TechWatch Report: Content Management Systems, available from: **www.jisc.ac.uk/ techwatch/reports/tsw_01-02.pdf**

[5]　W3C (2002): **www.w3c.org**

[6]　W3C WA1 (2002). Web Accessibility Initiative: **www.w3c.org/WAI**

[7]　Section 508 (2002), Section 508 the Road to accessibility **www.section508.gov/final_text.htm**

[8]　Macromedia (2002). Macromedia Resource Center, **www.macromedia.com/ macromedia/accessibility**

[9]　RNIB (2001), The status of Virtual Learning Environments with reference to accessibility for visually impaired people in the UK, November 2001, available from: **www.rnib.org.uk/technology/ articles.htm**

[10]　Adobe (2002a). Adobe Acrobat 5.0 Accessibility, **http://access.adobe.com/ acrobatmain.html**

[11]　Adobe (2002b). Adobe GoLive 6.0 Accessibility, **http://access.adobe.com/ golivemain.html**

[12]　Usablenet (2002). LIFT for Macromedia Dreamweaver **http://usablenet.com/ lift_dw?lift_dw.html** Date accessed 24/04/02

[13]　**www.cast.org/bobby**

[14]　W3C CSS (2002). W3C CSS Validation Service, **http://jigsaw.w3.org/ css-validator**

[15]　**thecounter.com**

9.12 Resources

[16]　Disability Rights Commission. (2002). The Disability Discrimination Act (1995): new requirements to make goods, facilities, services and premises more accessible to disabled people from 2004: New Code of Practice, available from: **www.drc-gb.org/drc/ InformationAndLegislation/Page331a.asp**

[17]　DfES (2002), Increase and Widen Participation in HE (The Excellence Challenge), available from: **www.dfee.gov.uk/excellencechallenge/ home**

[18]　HESA (2002), HESA online Information Service: available from: **www.hesa.ac.uk/ holisdocs/pubinfo/student/disab90.htm**

[19]　Office of the e-Envoy. (2002), Guidelines for UK Government Web sites, available from: **www.open.gov.uk/dev/neil**

[20]　SKILL (2002). Briefing sessions on the DDA/SENDA, available from: **www.skill.org.uk/news/dda_senda.htm**

Chapter 10

Dyslexia and Virtual Learning Environment Interfaces

Stuart Smith, MIMAS, University of Manchester

10.1 Introduction

As a widely recognised learning difficulty, dyslexia is likely to be covered by the UK Special Educational Needs and Disability Act (2001), which comes into effect September 2002. This chapter considers how institutions can comply with the Act and work to make their Virtual Learning Environments (VLEs) more accessible for dyslexic students. The results of a study that explored dyslexic students experience of using VLEs will be described along with the design and development of a new interface based on these results.

Before discussing the role of electronic media in teaching dyslexic students, it may be worthwhile to highlight some relevant information regarding dyslexia. The British Dyslexia Association (BDA) defines dyslexia as:

> "A specific difficulty in learning, constitutional in origin, in one or more of reading, spelling and written language, which may be accompanied by difficulty in number work. It is particularly related to mastering and using a written language (alphabetic, numerical and musical notation) although often affecting oral language to some degree." [1].

The BDA also states that about ten percent of the population have dyslexia [2]. Dyslexia seems to be caused by a physical condition of the brain [3] and appears to affect Short Term Memory (STM), giving rise to problems with sequencing [1,4]. STM is the ability of the mind to retain information for short periods of time before further processing either discards the information or stores it in the long-term memory [5]. The dyslexic fails to build an appropriate schema (a term used by psychologists to demonstrate how we bring separate skills together in order to conduct tasks which appear deceptively simple, such as writing) [4]. Sequencing controls almost all of our conscious actions, such as talking for example. Hence a condition that affects the ability to sequence effectively, such as dyslexia, can be potentially very debilitating. Sequencing can affect many different parts of the brain and is involved in different sensory channels. No two dyslexics' conditions manifest themselves in quite the same way [1].

For most people, the left side of the brain is dominant. Dyslexia is a condition caused by the dominance of the right side of the brain and is incurable. However, there are strengths as well as weaknesses to right-side-brain dominance. The difficulties of dyslexia arise from the construction of society and its reliance on left-brain activities, such as writing. There is nothing dyslexics can do to change their condition. Instead they must learn to cope effectively with the obstacles that society places before them. For example, some dyslexics use coloured screens to aid with their reading [1]. For its part, society must remove the barriers that dyslexics face, where possible. (See also Chapter 6 for an overview of the problems that dyslexic students cope with on a daily basis.)

10.2 Virtual Learning Environments

According to Stiles [6] Virtual Learning Environments (VLEs) "are online systems that provide collaborative interaction between tutors and students, and between students as peers, while also providing asynchronous learning resources for individualized use by students at any time". Work by Britain and Lieber [7] also supports Stiles' definition. They identify fifteen areas, which reflect the make-up of a VLE. These include items such as an email system, an assessment system, metadata (which is used to provide information about other data) and a navigation pathway.

Britain and Lieber make an interesting reference to the navigation pathway (or 'Navigation Model') in their assessment of VLEs, defining it as "… not strictly a feature or tool within a VLE, it is intrinsically part of the experience of using a VLE. The navigation facility allows a user to move around the environment and the navigation model or metaphor in conjunction with the look-and-feel of the system is extremely important as it defines in many ways how the system is used" [7].

Studying the VLE's impact on dyslexic users is beneficial since its navigation or interface governs the user's experience. Stiles in his definition of VLEs, makes the point that learning resources are available for the student's individual study [6]. So although VLEs are groupware they also have an important individual learning element and it is this element that I exploited in a study designed to consider the navigation of a learning resource within a VLE in an individual learning context.

10.3 Introducing COSE

The VLE chosen was a beta version of the Creation of Study Environments (COSE) tool. It was selected because some work on disability (including dyslexia) and accessibility within the COSE and Lotus Learning Space systems had been carried out previously by Stiles who is a Co-Director of the COSE project (See Figure 1 for a screenshot of COSE).

10.3.1 Testing the Interface

The navigation interface of the COSE VLE was tested using student volunteers, some of whom considered themselves dyslexic and some of whom did not. One of the problems of working with this study group is that anyone is potentially dyslexic and since not everyone is tested for the condition it is possible that they may never recognise the dyslexic tendencies in themselves. So, it is quite possible that there were unidentified dyslexics in the 'non-dyslexic' group.

After the COSE browser was tested, the following areas of the browser system were identified as causing particular difficulties for dyslexic users:

▶ In using the tutorial guide (written with Hypertext Mark-up Language, HTML), students have to leave the page in order to carry out a task that they are learning. When they return to continue with the tutorial, they are returned to the beginning of the HTML page they last used, not to the point on the page where they left. The user therefore has to remember their place in a lengthy sequence of words. This could prove difficult for a student with dyslexia.

▶ The COSE browser uses a navigation tree, which does not follow a hierarchical pattern of indentation (as in Microsoft Windows Explorer, for example). Certain elements within the navigation tree produce new branches from the root node rather than indented branches from the current node. This requires a user to keep careful track of their place on the tree, placing

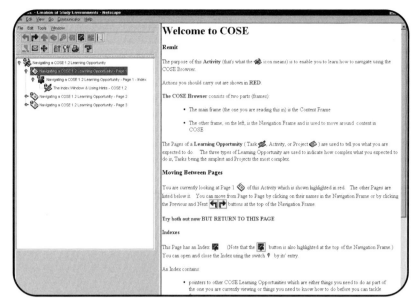

Figure 1: COSE
Browser screenshot

a demand on the STM. This may cause problems for a dyslexic user, as the user-testing confirmed. The issue was compounded by the fact that most users found the icons in the navigation tree difficult to comprehend.

▶ Several of the icons within the COSE browser are in the shape of similar jigsaw puzzle pieces. There is nothing unique to identify them other than colour. The user must remember the colour of the piece to identify the function of the jigsaw icon and the two (colour and function) may have no obvious connection. This design presents difficulties for all users, particularly those with dyslexia.

▶ The icons change in appearance between elements of the tutorial and browser. Users have to store up to three different designs for the same function in their STM when learning to use the system. So there is potential for confusion, especially for dyslexic users.

▶ The system relies on pop-up windows, which distract the dyslexic user's attention. Sometimes, the system produces a sequence of windows, which the user is forced to manage. This can be particularly problematic for dyslexic users.

▶ Many dyslexic users have trouble in reading and this is considered to be the primary manifestation of their disability [2]. Unfortunately, the COSE text of the programme guide is very long and inconsistently laid out. Perhaps, unsurprisingly, the length and layout of the tutorial text caused dyslexic users great difficulty during the interface testing.

10.4 Developing a new interface

We decided to experiment with a new approach towards developing of the VLE interface. This was based on IBM RealThings methodology, which takes objects from the real world and uses them as a related metaphor for a computerised system. The approach is attractive because it uses familiarity to construct the interface. The usefulness of familiarity in interface design is established in the literature [8]. It has another advantage for dyslexic users in that it uses established patterns of dealing with things rather than trying to create new ones. This should decrease the demands on the STM. However, it does rely on familiarity with the real world equivalent in the first instance.

RealThings, like the RealCD, are designed using the Object, View, and Interaction Design (OVID) approach [9]. OVID is an Object Orientated User Interface (OOUI) user-centred design approach. Objects are an interesting concept in user-interface design since their construction does not necessarily follow a hierarchy, although the objects must belong to a class and have relationships with one another.

Following the design process a three-dimensional (3D) navigation tool was created using Virtual Reality Modelling Language (VRML). This was used to navigate a tutorial developed for exploring the prototype 'world'. Up to this point, students had been user-testing the general interface of the software. The next stage was to test the software in a tutorial. The content chosen for the tutorial was a basic roast chicken recipe [10] (see Figure 2). Although the information within the interface

Figure 2: example screenshot from prototype interface

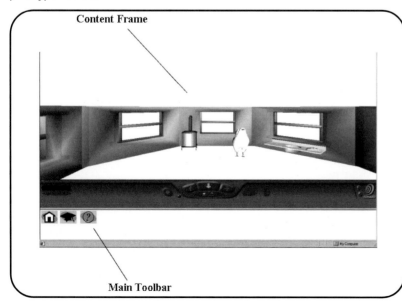

was related it was not hierarchical. Users were taken through a short introductory 'world', which led to background information about the learning environment. This allowed them the opportunity to become familiar with the navigation of the 'world' and the objects they would see. Once in the 'world' they were allowed to explore without restriction. Visual tools within the 'world' were used to guide the user, such as walls, which kept the user's attention focused on the area where the navigation objects were placed. There was no attempt to force users to visit the objects in any order. They were free to construct their own navigation schema from exploration and familiarisation.

Although not widely used, VRML provides a powerful prototyping tool for this kind of exercise. VRML coding allows sophisticated shading to provide better realism, which is important for increasing the familiar appearance of 3D objects displayed on a 2D device such as a monitor. It also allows the accurate placing of objects on screen. Importantly, it also allows links to be established between an object in the 3D interface and anything else. This could be another 'world', an HTML file, another Web site, a movie file or any number of items. This means that the interface produced was potentially very flexible. VRML 'worlds' can also be embedded into HTML.

From the analysis of the testing [11] two conclusions were drawn.

- the prototype interface can be considered dyslexic-friendly,
- the dyslexic-friendly prototype interface is not a hindrance to non-dyslexic users.

The adoption of an OOUI design approach seems to have produced an interface, which is appropriate for dyslexic and non-dyslexic users. However, the design methodology adopted, based on the OVID approach, is simply the tool for guiding the design of the interface. The interface concept itself has come from a consideration of the current understanding of dyslexia, the requirements of VLEs and the reactions of dyslexics and non-dyslexics to an existing VLE interface. The OVID design methodology and the influence of the RealThings approach have provided the means to represent a VLE interface in a more meaningful way to dyslexic users.

This design approach places an emphasis on understanding the needs of the user and it seems to have produced an interface that is appropriate for both dyslexic and non-dyslexic users (see Figure 3).

10.5 Conclusions

If user-testing were more widely deployed in both the academic and commercial world, the potential would exist to produce better all-round interfaces, assuming that the testing groups reflect society accurately. This should produce a more satisfactory product from the user's viewpoint. It should also decrease subsequent development costs of later versions of the software since the developers will have acquired an understanding of user requirements while user-testing previous versions.

10.6 References

[1]   Dayan, G. (1992), Clearing the Way, London, Booksprint.

[2]   British Dyslexia Association. (2001), What is dyslexia? Available from: **www.bda-dyslexia.org.uk/ d02adult/a01what.htm**

[3]   Brooks, L. (1997), Dyslexia: 100 Years on Brain Research and Understanding, available from: **www.dyslexia-inst.org.uk/ articles/100_years.htm**

[4]   Chasty, H. (1985), What is Dyslexia? A Developmental Language Perspective in Snowling, M.J (ed), Children's Written Language Difficulties: Assessment and Management, Windsor, Nfer-Nelson.

[5]   Eysenk, M. (1993), Principles of Cognitive Psychology, London, Taylor and Francis

[6]   Stiles, M. (2001), Staffordshire University Learning Development Centre and Disability Services, Disability Access To Virtual Learning Environments. DISinHE Study, available from: **www.disinhe.ac.uk/library/ print.asp?ID=41**

[7]   Britain, S. and Lieber, O. (2000), A Framework for the Pedagogical Evaluation of Virtual Learning Environments, JTAP Report No. 041, available from: **www.jisc.ac.uk:8080/jtap/htm/ jtap-041.html**

[8]   Dix, A. J., Finlay J. E., Abowd G. D. and Beale, R. (1998), Human-Computer Interaction, 2nd ed., Prentice Hall.

[9]   Roberts, D., Berry D., Isenee S. and Mullaly J. (1998), Designing for the User with OVID: Bridging User Interface Design and Software Engineering, Indianapolis, Macmillan Technical Publishing.

[10]   Lawrence, M., Ardley, S., MacMillan N., Murfitt, J., Nilsen, A., Maxwell, S., Eaton, J., Jones, B., Westland, P. and McHoy P. (1998), The Illustrated Hints Tips and Household Skills: The Practical, Step-By-Step Home Reference Manual, Avonmouth, Parragon.

[11]   Smith, S. (2001), Can a Virtual Learning Environment Interface Meet the Needs of Dyslexics and Non-Dyslexics?, (MSc Dissertation) Staffordshire University.

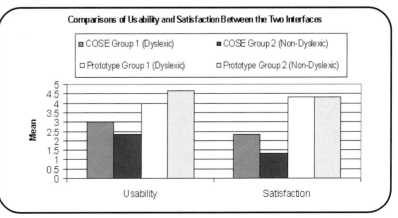

Figure 3: comparisons of usability and satisfaction between the two interfaces

Chapter 11

Towards accessible Virtual Learning Environments

Chris Cann, Educational Consultant
Simon Ball and **Allan Sutherland,** TechDis

11.1 Introduction

With the increasing use of Virtual Learning Environments (VLEs) in further and higher education, the Special Educational Needs and Disability Act (2001) (part 4 of the Disability Discrimination Act (1995)), which comes into force in September 2002, has particular relevance to developers and providers of VLEs. Developers and vendors can also help to ensure that VLEs are inclusive learning media by understanding the barriers that individuals face (whether or not they use assistive technology) and creating hardware and software designed to be accessible to all users. They should also understand the importance of designing accessible VLE content in order to provide guidance for users.

The same guidelines for designing Web pages (W3C WAI) to help ensure that disabled students and/or those with learning difficulties are not excluded can and should be applied to the use of VLEs. Institutions should make all their online learning materials, as well as their Web site material, accessible to disabled students and this means ensuring that the selected VLE is as accessible to users as possible. Users must also be given advice about how to create accessible learning materials within the VLEs.

Introducing accessibility issues into the decision-making and implementation stages is another important step in helping to ensure inclusive VLE learning media. With this in mind, TechDis undertook to provide information to educational institutions that have recently or are about to purchase a VLE. The research focused on the following VLEs and their accessibility to users: Blackboard, COSE, Granada Learnwise, Fretwell-Downing (FD) learning environment, Futuremedia Solstra, Teknical Virtual Campus and WebCT. These products were identified because they are part of the JISC inter-operability projects [1].

The project attempted to assess the approach and position of each of the above VLE vendors in relation to accessibility. A questionnaire was designed to explore each VLE vendor's approach to accessibility. The survey used W3C Priority 1 guidelines [2] to formulate the accessibility questions. This was circulated electronically to the seven VLE providers listed above and was followed-up by email reminders and telephone requests to complete and return the questionnaires.

The vendors were asked a series of questions regarding the provision within their organisation of an accessibility policy statement and accessibility advice, and their view on adherence to relevant guidelines. They were also asked about provision within their product of a series of accessibility features relating to general usage, image maps, tables, frames, applets and multimedia.

11.2 Survey findings

Summaries of the vendors corporate positions in relation to accessibility are as shown below.

Blackboard
▶ Blackboard has an accessibility policy statement and provides details on their Web site [3]. Their accessibility contact is Reidy Brown, rbrown@blackboard.com
▶ Blackboard has extensive accessibility information for product users on their Web site [4]
▶ Blackboard actively pursue adherence to the W3C WAI Web Content, Authoring Tool and User Agent Accessibility Guidelines.

COSE
▶ COSE is in the final phase of development prior to the release of version 2.0. The bulk of accessibility work will take place immediately after the release of version 2.0 [5]
▶ COSE does not have an accessibility policy statement as yet but will prepare one to coincide with the release of an accessible system
▶ COSE is a Java applet, and their view is that both the applet itself and the HTML content created by the users should be accessible.

FD Learning Environment (le)

▶ FD has an accessibility policy statement. It is currently not on their Web site but can be made available on request

▶ FD is willing to provide advice on accessibility and their representative can be reached by email at info@fdlearning.com

▶ FD is working towards ensuring that their software complies with emerging industry guidelines on accessibility, as embodied by W3C WAI.

Futuremedia Solstra

▶ Futuremedia have not provided a response to the questionnaire or any alternative information.

Granada LearnWise

▶ LearnWise has an accessibility statement, which can be accessed via their Web site [6]

▶ LearnWise provides advice on accessibility via their support helpline service and a separate service called SIS (Semerc Information Service). Both of these can be accessed via support@learnwise.net

▶ LearnWise currently implements several features designed to improve accessibility including an adaptable interface/function set and a built-in text-to-speech engine.

Teknical

Teknical did not complete the questionnaire but in a letter from their Chief Executive, Professor Jack Adams, they made the following points:

▶ "A very large proportion of our R&D spend is targeted towards compliance with both current and developing standards and legislation, which support improved accessibility"

▶ "The information that we would like under the Teknical response would be 'Please contact Teknical or see our Web site for information about products and services'" [7].

WebCT

▶ WebCT has an accessibility policy statement, offers advice on accessibility for users, and provides a contact person for further advice. Details can be found on the WebCT Web site [8].

▶ WebCT supports the Section 508 regulations. (In 1998, the US Congress amended the Rehabilitation Act to require federal agencies to make their electronic and information technology accessible to people with disabilities [9].)

11.3 Conclusion

A range of guidelines and checklists are available to aid accessibility and to ensure that VLEs are inclusive rather than exclusive. The research suggests that US vendors (Blackboard and WebCT) have made strong commitments to improving the accessibility of their products in response to the legislative requirements of Section 508. However, UK vendors (COSE, FD learning environment and LearnWise) have also made recent strides towards accessibility as can be seen in their corporate policies. They are currently working on programming issues and guidance to users.

TechDis are working with the Royal National College for the Blind in Hereford on user-testing of VLEs with students who have a range of disabilities and learning difficulties. The results of this project will be available in September and will supplement these findings.

Finally, the research highlights the need for providers to address accessibility issues in light of current UK legislation and for institutions to consider the accessibility of a VLE as a contributing factor when purchasing and implementing a VLE. It is essential that institutions that have already purchased a VLE continue to work with vendors to ensure that equal accessibility for all users remains a high priority.

11.4 References

[1] www.jisc.ac.uk/mle/interop/interop-reports.html
[2] www.w3.org/TR/WAI-WEBCONTENT/full-checklist.html
[3] http://products.blackboard.com/cp/bb5/access/index.cgi
[4] http://products.blackboard.com/cp/bb5/access/508coursebuilders.cgi
[5] www.staffs.ac.uk/COSE
[6] www.learnwise.net/products/server_accessibility.jhtml
[7] www.teknical.com
[8] http://www.webct.com/products/viewpage?name=products_accessibility
[9] More information about Section 508 can be found at www.section508.gov

Improving staff awareness of accessibility legislation for online teaching and learning materials: a case study

Susi Peacock, Daniel Ross and **Jacqui Skelton**, Queen Margaret University College

12.1 Introduction

Recent legislation in the United Kingdom, including the Special Educational Needs and Disabilities Act 2001 (SENDA), as well as the Quality Assurance Agency (QAA) Code of Practice concerning disabled students [1], has significantly impacted on the learning and teaching environment in post-16 education. One of the key barriers for institutions is the lack of staff awareness with regard to accessibility, which is compounded by a resource-scarce environment: lack of time and money. This chapter describes the development and planned deployment of a module in a Virtual Learning Environment (VLE) at Queen Margaret University College (QMUC), Edinburgh. This is part of the University College's response to the legislation. The module aims to provide for staff an overview of the legislation with regard to online learning materials. Two groups have been fundamental in the development of this module. As part of a JISC-funded project, QMUC has a Roundtable. This is a special group drawn from all sectors of the institution empowered to support the meaningful deployment of learning technologies at QMUC. In addition, QMUC has developed a devolved system of support for disabled students through departmental Special Needs Co-ordinators (SNCs) and Support Service Co-ordinators (SSCs). They liaise with relevant teaching and support staff to ensure specific student needs are being met.

12.2 The institutional context: Queen Margaret University College

QMUC seeks to become Edinburgh's fourth university and in 2000 had the highest graduate employment rate in Scotland (84%) [2]. It has approximately 3200 full-time students and 1100 part-time; 222 students (5.2%) at QMUC have registered disabilities:

Disability	Students
dyslexia	78
blind/partially sighted	10
deaf/hearing impairment	13
wheelchair user/mobility difficulties	3
mental health difficulties	3
an unseen disability e.g. diabetes, epilepsy, asthma	84
multiple disabilities	6
a disability not listed above	25
TOTAL	222

Table 1: a break down of the range of student disabilities at QMUC

A number of initiatives already exist at QMUC to improve access and support for special needs students. These include a new access centre in the Library, which was recently opened and named after a particularly tenacious student in recognition of her constant campaigning to improve facilities for blind students. In addition, Special Needs Co-ordinators and Support Service Co-ordinators provide information, guidance and support for disabled students throughout their time at QMUC. SNCs and SSCs help students draw up Individual Learning Plans (ILPs) specific to the student's learning and teaching, examination and assessment needs and play a key role in disseminating this information to colleagues. Specialist training is offered to SNCs and SSCs and will shortly be delivered to admissions staff to ensure the Institution is fully prepared at the pre-entry stage and can offer a realistic support and academic package to disabled students. This system, although still in the early stages, has provided a much-needed structure with regards to identification and monitoring of both the Institution and the students progress and helps to highlight resource and development issues.

Like most further and higher education institutions, at QMUC there is a growth in the development of online materials for learning and teaching. Most of these materials are for 'blended learning' where online resources enhance and enrich traditional delivery [3]. The Web pages usually consist of extra materials, resources, links to Web sites, case studies, diagrams, PowerPoint Presentations and Frequently Asked Questions lists. In addition, approximately 100 modules have been incorporated into QMUC's VLE (WebCT). These modules include the development of content as well as the use of interactive tools, for example, online discussions and quizzes and support both 'blended' and fully online modules.

The deployment of learning technologies at QMUC is supported and directed by a Roundtable. This special group was established as part of a JISC-funded project to trial the American Association for Higher Education's Teaching, Learning and Technology Group's Roundtable Methodology [4,5]. A Roundtable brings together on a regular basis a wide-ranging group of individuals including librarians, academic staff, technology professionals, students and administrative staff. At QMUC, the Roundtable has developed recommendations to enhance teaching and learning through technology and improved communication and collaboration amongst its members and across the institution. Central to the workings of a Roundtable is the establishment of working groups that focus on specific areas and work to fulfil the mission and vision of an institution's Roundtable. At each meeting, the working groups report on progress, actual and perceived barriers and discuss the way forward in consultation with other members of the group.

The co-chairs of the Roundtable were aware of the increased use of online materials and the VLE at QMUC. Although promising to enhance access for many of our students, the co-chairs suspected that the lecturers creating Web pages and using the VLE had little, if any, knowledge of the impact of the new accessibility legislation. Furthermore, the co-chairs were aware that without the proper staff support and training, many of those online materials could be more of a hindrance than help for disabled students. The co-chairs therefore agreed that a working group in the Roundtable would focus on improving staff awareness in this area.

The working group consisted of two members of the Roundtable (an information technology specialist and a staff developer) plus a faculty librarian with a specific interest in special needs,

the WebCT Administrator and the Student Disability Advisor. They worked together to develop a WebCT module, which aims at improving staff awareness and providing practical support in developing accessible online materials. WebCT was chosen as the appropriate training medium because staff requiring information about making online materials accessible are already familiar with the Web and QMUC's VLE. In addition, WebCT would provide a rapid and easy mechanism for updating and expanding materials as appropriate. The module would also be able to demonstrate potential opportunities for staff using WebCT. WebCT version 3.6 and onwards was developed with the section 508, American Disabilities Act very much in mind. WebCT also collaborated with Freedom Scientific (the makers of JAWS screen reader) to ensure that the product was accessible [6]. Although WebCT uses frames, it is compliant with current QMUC recommended guidelines, but this does not include any materials that are imported into it.

12.3 Development of a staff development module in a Virtual Learning Environment

The WebCT module consists of two content sections, a set of compiled resources and an introductory video and guide. Throughout there are interactive links to the glossary, quizzes and other resources (See Figure 1).

The first of the two content modules (see Figure 2) explains the significance of the legislation for lecturing and support staff. It describes QMUC's current situation, resources and provisions for special needs students. Details of SNCs, SSCs, their responsibilities and remits are included in the module. There is an in-house video with subtitles of two of QMUC's disabled students that highlights the problems faced by these students in an environment that is still moving towards full compliance with accessibility legislation. This is followed by a review of online resources including suppliers of technology, information Web sites, guides and techniques for creating accessible materials. The changes required to create accessible resources are then addressed. There are links to the 'Do-It Resources' at the University of Washington, US [7] and UK case studies that look at practical examples of the legislation [8]. This covers not only the creation of accessible materials, but also the planning of an accessible curriculum. Finally, the module addresses required policy changes and recommendations for future developments at QMUC.

The second of the two content modules provides a simple set of techniques and guidelines (see Figure 3) for the staff producing online teaching and learning materials derived from the Web Accessibility Initiative (WAI) guidelines [9]. These guidelines also include links to several online formative and summative quizzes that allow staff to check their understanding of the techniques and the concepts behind them. The two content modules are based on a wide variety of resources and include journal articles, books, Web sites, reports and emails. There are already many Web sites that deal with disabilities in education. Some of the most useful include the University of Aberdeen's guidelines for academic staff [10], the Web accessibility initiative and the University of Washington's 'Do-It Resources' (including video resources). Other helpful resources include TechDis [11], CAST [12] and the Disabled Rights Commission [13] as well as articles published by the DisInHE project (now transferred to TechDis).

12.4 Evaluation of the module

After the initial development of the WebCT Module, there was extensive evaluation through the Roundtable, SNCs and SSCs. Feedback in the form of a questionnaire was provided from technology professionals, academics, students, librarians and TechDis. Several individuals also kindly offered face to face feedback as well.

In general, the evaluation was very positive:

"Excellent resource for those making Web pages"
"Very useful resource."
"Excellent beginning [but] will need to be continually updated."
"Makes me very keen to get to grips with WebCT."

The design and content of the module were highly praised especially the guidelines, student interviews and quizzes. None of the evaluators perceived WebCT as a barrier to staff training. Four areas of concern, however, arose through the evaluation:

▶ lack of Windows Media Player video codecs and QuickTime players on staff PCs meant that many of our evaluators were initially unable to view the videos. Although this is still a problem, a key member of ITC is involved with the

Roundtable and is assisting the deployment of these in the future
▶ time taken to create subtitles for in-house videos. The addition of the subtitles was complicated and very time-consuming especially because it required detailed editing due to the lack of access to sophisticated software. This will unfortunately remain the situation at QMUC especially since outsourcing will not be an option
▶ accessibility of WebCT self-test tool. The self-test tool uses frames, one for the question and one for the feedback. This means that a screen reader is unlikely to notice that the contents of the feedback frame have changed when an answer is selected. The self-tests were, therefore, converted to standard quizzes
▶ focus of the module. Several evaluators suggested further materials that could be incorporated into the module which were related materials but not fundamental to online materials. Some of this material has been included as additional resources but others will be made available to staff through alternative training events.

Currently the WebCT module does not have a discussion forum. For the future, this facility could allow all those with access to the module to post technical questions or general queries, which could be responded to by other members of the QMUC community. Depending on the amount and frequency of access, there are several options by which an online discussion group can be formed. The discussion tool within WebCT could be implemented but this would limit responses to a closed group, with little chance of increased participation and input from participants outside of QMUC. Alternatively a link to an existing email group could be established, providing access to a wider user group, with the opportunity to increase in size and scope.

12.5 Deployment of the module

The next challenge is the effective deployment of the module to all appropriate staff in the institution. As one of our evaluators stated:

"The worry is that IT-phobic staff will not access this resource."

A number of disability-related initiatives will be launched in the coming months that will involve the WebCT module. These include:

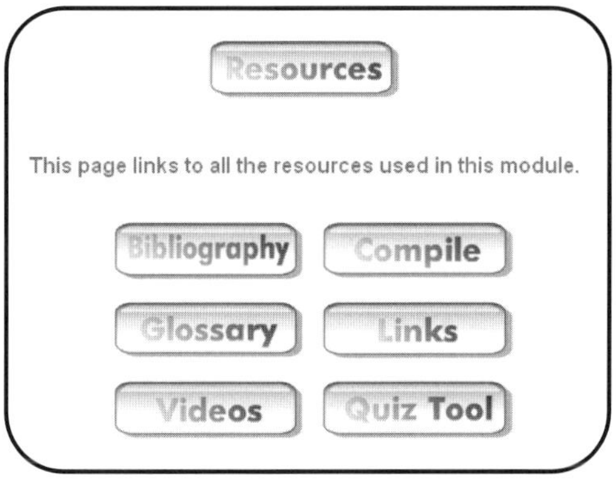

Figure 1:
resources page

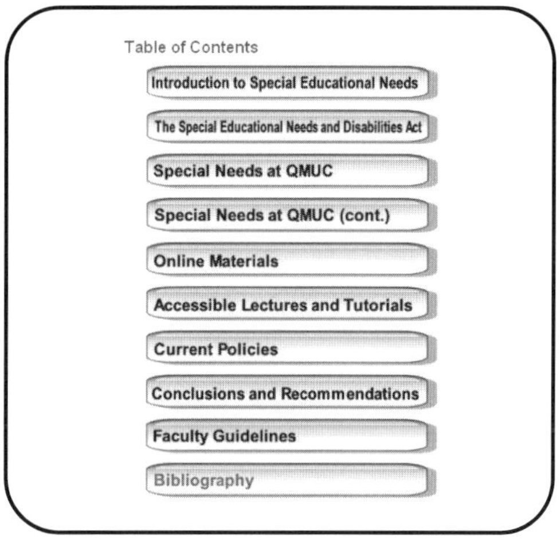

Figure 2: the first
content section in the
WebCT module

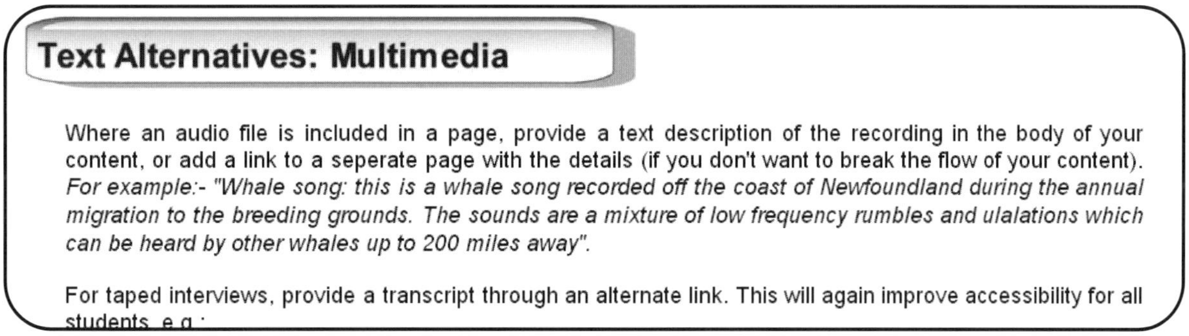

Figure 3:
guidelines
for
developing
Multimedia

Text Alternatives: Multimedia

Where an audio file is included in a page, provide a text description of the recording in the body of your content, or add a link to a seperate page with the details (if you don't want to break the flow of your content). *For example:- "Whale song: this is a whale song recorded off the coast of Newfoundland during the annual migration to the breeding grounds. The sounds are a mixture of low frequency rumbles and ulalations which can be heard by other whales up to 200 miles away".*

For taped interviews, provide a transcript through an alternate link. This will again improve accessibility for all students, e.g.:

▶ a new institutional disability policy which will be issued to all staff. This will contain resource materials and a signpost to the module. In addition, at the launch of the policy, there will be a demonstration of the WebCT module

▶ general disability awareness training including an introduction to the module for all staff, will take place across the institution in the near future. This will be integrated into new staff inductions

▶ specialist workshops for SNCs and SSCs including the module which will be provided as continuing development

▶ encouragement by the learning technology advisor and WebCT Administrator to all staff using the VLE and developing Web pages to access the module and complete the summative quiz.

The Roundtable and SNCs will continue to raise awareness and actively encourage others in their departments and across the institution to access the module. The Dean of Learning and Teaching has provided a small gift for the first five to successfully complete the summative quizzes. In addition, in the forthcoming academic year, there will be a special presentation to QMUC's Management Team by co-chair of the Roundtable.

12.6 Conclusion

It is the intention that the WebCT module at QMUC will be widely used by staff involved in the development of online materials. As always the enthusiasts will be keen to access the module but it is essential that all those involved with Web page and VLE module creation have a thorough understanding of the legislation and their responsibility. The evaluation suggests that WebCT, in this case, will not be a barrier to staff training. Two groups have been fundamental to the success of the development and evaluation of the module and they will undoubtedly play a crucial role in its deployment across the institution. The first of these is QMUC's Roundtable: a cross-institutional group, which has supported the initiative and will play a crucial role in further promoting the module. In addition, the SNCs, the SSCs and their Co-ordinators, the Disability Advisor and the Wider Participation and Development Officer, have provided vital feedback, enthusiasm and an ongoing commitment. They will be essential in the deployment of the module in the coming months.

12.7 References

[1] QAA Code of Practice for Students with Disabilities, available from: **www.qaa.ac.uk/public/COP/COPswd/contents.htm**

[2] **www.qmuc.ac.uk/welcome.htm**

[3] Smith, J. (2001), "Blended Learning. An Old Friend gets a New Name." Executive Update Online, available from: **www.gwsae.org/ExecutiveUpdate/2001/March/blended.htm**

[4] Further information about this JISC-funded project is available at: **www.roundtable.ac.uk**

[5] The Teaching and Learning Technology Group has developed the Roundtable Methodology. It is part of the American Association for Higher Education. Further materials are available at: **www.tltgroup.org**

[6] JAWS is currently the most popular screen reader world-wide: **www.freedomscientific.com/fs_products/software_jaws.asp**

[7] The Disabilities, Opportunities, Internet-working, and Technology Project at the University of Washington provides a tremendous resource of relevant materials despite slight differences in the US and UK legislation: **www.washington.edu/doit**

[8] Disability Draft Code of Practice (post-16): **www.drc-gb.org/drc/documents/Post16CoP.pdf**

[9] World Accessibility Initiative Web site: **www.w3c.org/WAI/Resources/#te**

[10] University of Aberdeen Web site, which has a range of high-quality resources **www.abdn.ac.uk/diss/ltu/accessibility/index.hti**

[11] **www.techdis.ac.uk**

[12] CAST is an educational, not-for-profit organization. It uses technology to expand opportunities for all people, including those with disabilities: **www.cast.org**

[13] Disability Rights Commission Web site: **www.drc.org.uk/drc/default.asp**

Acknowledgements

The authors would like to thank QMUC's Roundtable, Special Needs Co-ordinators, Support Services Co-ordinators, Chris Cook, Alison Kilgour, Mark Wilkinson, Liam Nelson, Rosita Green and TechDis

Accessibility and computer-based assessment: a whole new set of issues?

Chapter 13

Kathy Wiles, LTSN Generic Centre

13.1 Introduction

"...disabled students are an integral part of the academic community... accessible and appropriate provision is not 'additional' but a core element of the overall service which an institution makes available." [1]

Assessment is central to the learning experience, and much is currently being done to integrate assessment within online and computer-based learning. The Disability Discrimination Act (1995) lists examinations and assessments as services that further and higher education institutions must provide without discriminating against disabled people [2]. While debate continues about the level of assessment that can be automated and whether deep or higher-order learning can be assessed online, little is being said about accessibility issues raised by the increased use of automated and online assessment. What are the accessibility issues? Is computer-based assessment an aid or a hindrance to accessibility? Are online assessments being designed with accessibility in mind or is there a danger of excluding individuals who may be enabled to participate in accredited education through online assessment? Assessments are the high-stakes, high-risk part of the educational process; should a stricter standard of accessibility be applied? This chapter looks at some of these issues and is intended to stimulate debate and to initiate further work in this area.

13.1 Outlining the accessibility issues that computer-based assessments raise

Online learning offers many opportunities both for widening participation in and increasing access to learning for disabled students. Assistive technologies and the removal of the requirement to physically attend the classroom have the potential to break down many barriers confronting disabled students in the world of

further and higher education. Much has been done to educate teachers in the design of accessible and inclusive teaching materials. However, in the area of computer-based and online assessment, there is little tangible evidence that guidelines for inclusive and accessible design are emerging [3]. This chapter attempts to highlight the deficit of such guidelines and to identify some of the issues that may arise in using computer-based assessment for disabled students.

For the sake of clarity, it's worth quickly reviewing what computer-based assessment means. While this phrase certainly includes computer-aided assessment, it can also include assessment that is facilitated electronically, such as assignments delivered by email, marked contributions to online discussions, or the use of videoconferencing and virtually-created situations. Computer-aided assessment itself covers a broad range of tools from automated multiple-choice type questions to the use of media, simulations and virtual laboratory spaces for testing students. Thus, where sound, vision, dexterity, the ability to spell words 'correctly' and speedy response times can affect the outcome of assessments; accessibility issues must also be considered and explored. There is no doubt that computer-based assessment offers many opportunities to improve accessibility for students. A student with a visual impairment equipped with a screen reader, headphones and well-designed assessment can be assessed in the same laboratory as his or her fellow students, eliminating the need for a separate room, a dedicated invigilator and an assistant to read the examination script or to transcribe material. Information Technology and inclusive design provide an opportunity to develop new ways of assessing our students. The use of videos, videoconferencing and streaming audio can enhance the assessment (as well as the learning) experience for all students while removing accessibility barriers. Assistive technologies continue to develop and many are now widely available [4]. While they can help to resolve some accessibility issues, they also introduce the potential for new difficulties in assessment. To avoid these:

- the teacher must understand how the assistive technology can be used,
- the student must be familiar with using the technology itself. Introducing assistive technology to students with an exam deadline looming would place an added learning cost on the student,
- it may be necessary to verify assistive technology through internal auditing and verification systems before it can be used in an examination situation.

There are other concerns related to computer-based assessment with teachers.

13.1.1 Multiple-Choice Questions
The most commonly used online assessment tool in UK higher education is the multiple-choice question (MCQ) and its variants (gap-filling, sequencing, etc.). This tool is available as a standalone system or can be found as one of the range of tools offered within proprietary Virtual Learning Environments (VLEs) (hence its popularity). There are a number of accessibility issues related to the use of MCQs:

- for visually-impaired students who rely on text-to-speech software, remembering a variety of spoken information can require considerable mental effort [5]
- students who rely on text-to-speech software require greater time to acquire and digest information than students who can visually read the data
- MCQs often offer very subtle distinctions between choices. Visually-impaired students are likely to need longer to determine these distinctions. A dyslexic student may be unable to identify such subtle distinctions
- MCQs that address higher-order understanding rather than surface learning are very complex and can require numerous re-readings. This has the potential to disadvantage the visually-impaired student and those using text-to-speech software
- progressing between options using the tab key (for students who cannot use a mouse) can take up a great deal of additional time.

13.1.2 Text-Searching/Matching
It is possible to use an assessment tool that searches for certain key words in the text which are then matched to a pre-suggested list set by

the teacher to gauge whether students have used the kind of stock vocabulary one would expect from the subject matter set. What if the correct words appear but are misspelled? Are we in danger of measuring spelling rather than understanding? This issue can be applied equally to all students of course, but it holds a particular relevance for dyslexic students. Recent developments in highlighting the needs of dyslexic students in education could easily be reversed by less than careful analysis of what we test our students on and the methodology we choose to evidence this.

13.1.3 Automated Transition
Computer-based assessment tools are advancing in their level of sophistication and automation. Many now offer automatic transition from question to question after a certain amount of time has elapsed, even if the student has not attempted to answer the question. This method is used widely in testing IT skills, for example in European Computer Driving Licence testing software, where students are allotted a certain amount of time to complete questions. Although students can choose to move to the next question whenever they please, there is no method of slowing down the transition between questions if a user needs more time. While it is possible to set times for tests independently within VLEs, teachers and learning technologists must be aware of issues to do with timing when investing in proprietary testing software.

13.1.4 Online Discussions
One way of insuring that students participate in online discussions is to mark their contributions. The use of discussion is seen as one of the best ways of using online tools to enhance the learning experience and enhance accessibility to disabled students. However, assessing contributions to discussions requires the facilitator/tutor to consider several issues:

- in synchronous discussion, account must be taken of how quickly students are expected to respond. In large discussions, threads build up very quickly and discussion moves on rapidly. For students who rely on screen readers or who do not have mouse dexterity, contributing in real time is a significant issue. If students believe that the discussion has moved on by the time they are ready to make their contribution, they may feel too shy to contribute. Assimilating the threads in synchronous discussion can also be extremely challenging: how does a student know, for example, how far a particular thread of the discussion and the discussion itself have progressed? How does the visually-impaired student know that a point which has arisen for them from a message is not raised one or two messages further down? Should a visually-impaired student feel obliged to listen to and assimilate all messages before contributing or responding? And, if they are following a particular thread and someone responds to their contribution, how can this be brought to their attention?

▶ when discussion is asynchronous, fewer barriers to accessibility are immediately obvious. However, asynchrous discussion raises questions regarding the assimilation of the threads of discussion and awareness of when discourse has begun and ended.

These issues clearly create the potential for disabled students to be treated less favourably than other students. Indeed, the Draft Code of Practice for Post-16 provision of education duties specifically cites as an example of placing at a 'substantial disadvantage' a student who is unable to take part in an online discussion and therefore loses marks [6]. This is one of the few specific references to the accessibility of online assessment in current legislation and publicly-available guidelines.

13.2 Legislation and codes of practice

Has the message of inclusive design in computer-based assessment been delivered effectively? The Special Educational Needs and Disability Act (2001) [7], (which brings education within the remit of the DDA (1995)) and the British Standards Institution (BSI) standard BS 7988 (available in 2002) do not elaborate specifically on assessing disabled students and it has not been possible to determine specific guidelines in this area.

While BS 7988 includes the requirement to ensure 'that computer exams don't disadvantage people with special needs', it makes more reference to measures to stop so-called cyber-cheating than to designing assessments for accessibility. Indeed, its requirements for verification of the user's identity may create rather than remove barriers for disabled students [8]. However, the final wording of the standard may offer clearer guidance on the accessibility of online assessment than either SENDA or the QAA Code of Practice.

The various guidelines relating to examination and assessment assume that inclusive course design will automatically include good computer-based assessment design. Yet how we perceive and conduct assessments is very different from how everyday learning and teaching is designed. Issues highlighted in the computer-based examination and assessment process include: verification of student identity, specific time and location of assessment. These can all hinder the inclusion of disabled students in the online world.

13.3 Further development

While material is becoming available to advise both teachers and students on accessibility in more traditional examination formats (i.e., in an examination hall, through written examinations) [9], it has not been possible to find guidelines specifically for computer-based or online assessment. In writing this chapter a few tips and pointers have come to mind. Additions to this list would be very welcome, as a guide to designing for accessibility in computer-based assessment is much needed. This is an open invitation to the education community to contribute to the guide by submitting your suggestions by email to helpdesk@techdis.ac.uk. TechDis hopes to compile your suggestions into an 'accessibility in computer-based assessment' guide. In the meantime, here are a few suggestions:

▶ when designing multiple choice questions, try to avoid overly-complex answers, especially long lists with distinctions that can only be made by careful re-readings.

▶ if using graphics, ensure that high-quality recorded descriptions are available for each graphic used or that a narrative is included with video clips to describe any action taking place.

▶ allow students to set their own transition times between questions (but bear in mind that extra time may make the total exam burden more onerous) [10].

▶ allow students to navigate between questions using the keyboard rather than a mouse.

▶ if you use assistive technology to make the assessment more accessible, ask yourself if the student is being required to learn to use new technology at short notice, and whether this constitutes fair treatment.

▶ ask the advice of disabled students and use that feedback in the design of computer-based assessments. No one is better placed to advise on accessibility than disabled students who often have a great deal of experience and many useful contributions to make to the design of materials.

13.4 Conclusion

Many institutions make alternative arrangements for the assessment of disabled students as a matter of course and express this within their education policy. Guidelines for designing assessment for disabled students are beginning to emerge and some of these guidelines are transferable to computer-based assessment. However, it is important to remember that there is little benefit to disabled students in increasing the options for accessibility through computer-based and online learning and then removing that enhancement in assessing or examining the disabled student by not designing the computer-based assessment inclusively. A more radical approach is required, where disabled students do not require special treatment but can benefit from inclusively-designed equipment to go through the same educational processes and experiences as other students. While modifications to the examination and assessment processes are the only solution for accommodating disabled students, it is inevitable that barriers to their full and equal participation in further and higher education will continue to exist.

It may seem that the same issues of designing for accessibility apply also to any online learning materials, but complacency in the design of assessment presents a real danger. Webb suggests that accessibility should be considered at the start of the design process to reduce costs, though this can also reduce the need to continually revisit assessments and to adjust them for different levels of accessibility [11]. Arguably, getting assessment design wrong carries a higher risk, since students only get one chance at assessment whereas a lecturer will have the opportunity to modify learning materials over time. Other issues relate more specifically to assessment, such as the complexity of multiple-choice options and the amount of time available to answer questions, especially where automated transition or fixed timings for questions is used.

Computer and information technologies offer teachers and learning technologists an opportunity to implement 'inclusive design' in learning, teaching and assessment materials. Inclusive

design means that all students are accommodated, minimising exceptions or special arrangements where possible. In our attempts to diversify the assessment experience, we must not risk excluding some students through inattention to inclusive design issues. We must not fall into the trap of allowing innovation in technology to outstrip its usefulness as a tool that enables accessibility and assessment. Innovation is not necessarily an advancement if it is not accessible. Both SENDA and BS 7988 standard are missed opportunities to offer teachers some guidelines on computer-based assessment design. In light of the increasing use of communication and information technologies to facilitate access to education, this oversight is surprising and must be addressed.

13.5 References

[1]　The Quality Assurance Agency for Higher Education, (1999), Code of practice for the assurance of academic quality and standards in higher education: Section 3: Students with Disabilities, available from: **www.qaa.ac.uk/ public/COP/codesof-practice.htm**

[2]　DDA 1995 Act Available from: **www.legislation.hmso.gov.uk/acts/acts1995/Ukpga_19950050_en_1.htm**

[3]　See **www.questionmark.com/perception/help/articles/access/index.html** for some basic pointers on using HTML

[4]　See the TechDis Accessibility database available from: **www.techdis.ac.uk/access.html**

[5]　Luke, R. (2000), AccessAbility: Enabling technology for life long learning inclusion in an electronic classroom, Educational Technology and Society, 5 (1)

[6]　**www.drc-gb.org/drc/InformationAndLegislation/Page34A.asp**

[7]　Available from: **www.legislation.hmso.gov.uk/acts/acts2001/20010010.htm**

[8]　British Standards Institution, (2001), New exam guidelines to stop the cyber-cheats: Press Release, available from: **www.bsi-global.com/About+BSI/News+Room/exams.xalter**

[9]　For example **http://www.rnib.org.uk/student/exams.htm** and **www.ispn.gcal.ac.uk/teachability/Resources/Assessments.html**

[10] See Cowork project available from:
      **www.cowork.ac.uk/development/
      materials/assessment/coventry.htm**

[11] Webb, I. (1999), Accessibility and learning
      technology, available from:
      **www.techdis.ac.uk/resources/
      webb01.html**

13.6 Resources

[12] The Computer-Assisted Assessment Unit
      based at Loughborough University
      www.lboro.ac.uk/service/ltd/flicaa

[13] The Teachability project based at Glasgow
      Caledonian University aims to assist in
      creating an accessible curriculum for
      disabled students:
      www.ispn.gcal.ac.uk/teachability

[14] The CAA Centre was part of the Implemen-
      tation and Evaluation of Computer-assisted
      Assessment project and although the Web
      site is no longer maintained some resources
      are still useable and relevant:
      www.caacentre.ac.uk

Chapter 14

E-tutoring disabled students

Shirley Evans, Royal National College for the Blind

14.1 Introduction

This chapter examines the experience of e-tutoring disabled students at the Royal National College for the Blind (RNC) in Hereford. It will investigate e-tutoring in the context of the research and development carried out by the RNC's IT and learning body, ILT/ICT Task Force, as well as more general issues. We hope that readers will apply some of the ideas and solutions to their own institutions. The work so far has focused on blended e-learning, which is e-learning comple-mented by face-to-face tuition and carried out within the College. However, there are plans to extend this work to the distance-learning programme which uses significantly less 'traditional teaching'. Clearly, this has implications for staff development, and this chapter will consider the way in which the RNC is addressing this very important issue. The chapter will conclude with a look at how technological developments may affect e-tutoring over the next five years and how this relates to plans for future developments at RNC.

14.2 Research and development

The ILT/ICT Task Force was created in September 2000 with a remit to design and deliver an integrated learning and teaching package of training and support specifically to meet the IT needs of blind and partially-sighted individuals preparing for study and transition to employ-ment. The Task Force began by investigating Virtual Learning Environments (VLEs) and developing the RNC intranet. The initial aim was to purchase a VLE for College-wide use with the intranet as a tool to rationalise the RNC curriculum and as a stepping-stone to a VLE. It was only in the last year that the Task Force found any VLEs that students can access with screen readers, but these proved difficult to use. The need to prepare students to use the VLEs they might encounter in a less specialised further or higher education institution soon became clear. The Task Force has been assessing e-content and in particular trialling the National Learning Network materials (NLN) for accessibility. The College has prioritised the trialling and will work

closely with NLN as they produce the next round of materials. Developers will be consulting the Task Force before they begin building the materials and will also visit the College to understand better some of the issues that need to be addressed.

14.2.1 E-tutoring Pilots
The Task Force has been introducing e-learning to students in the past six months and some of the experiences of this process are set out below.

The Electronic Soap Group was set up within the Blackboard VLE to help deliver transitional skills to students aged sixteen to nineteen. The central idea was to use the discussion board in Blackboard to explore issues such as teenage pregnancy and drugs using a framework of a popular TV soap opera. The pilot lasted six weeks and included a one-and-a-half hour, face-to-face session each week. Students were expected to carry out assignments and to participate in the discussion board outside of the scheduled face-to-face sessions. Initial concerns that this might encourage students to become isolated appear unfounded. In fact, results show that this format enhances students' communication skills in the face-to-face environment. Six students participated in the Soap Group last term and will continue using the WebCT VLE this term.

Business Studies, Music Technology and Remedial Therapy materials have been posted to Blackboard and to WebCT, and these material will be developed ready for the next academic year. These two VLEs have been compared for their accessibility and usability, both from the students' and the tutors' perspectives. Research on these and other VLEs will be used by the Task Force in preparing advice notes for TechDis [1].

14.3 Some problems and solutions

The Task Force has been working with students whose disabilities include visual, hearing and motor impairments as well as dyslexia.

14.3.1 Hearing and/or mobility impaired students

So far deaf or hard-of-hearing students have not encountered barriers in using VLEs. Indeed, students have spoken enthusiastically about the experience of engaging in a discussion without having to worry about whether they missed something. The learning experience has been further enhanced by the provision of online text support in the NLN materials.

Students with motor impairments have experienced difficulties in accessing electronic content where keystroke options were not available and consequently mouse actions were the only options. For deaf, hard-of-hearing and mobility-impaired students the IMS Guidelines for Developing Accessible Learning Applications are a useful resource and provide further information and references [2].

14.3.2 Blind students

- It is difficult for students to use software intuitively. Simplicity and predictability are essential. In many cases students have to memorise navigational paths.
- While VLEs have been generally accessible with keystroke options and screen readers, they do have some limitations. For example, extensive use has been made in the study of the discussion board facility in Blackboard. Yet there is no facility (at the moment) for book-marking a page, or for generating an email alert when a message has been posted to the discussion board. Students must access the discussion board to check if a message has been posted to the board. This is a lengthy and laborious process. Moreover, messages are sorted according to date, which means that the most recent message is at the bottom of the list. This incurs substantial time and effort in navigation, especially with screen readers.
- Students need to be experienced in the use of screen readers. For example they will have to change cursor modes to do an online quiz and use forms mode to log in.
- Some materials have a text alternative, which can be useful, though this should not be regarded as an alternative for blind students. While it is a relatively simple task to create accessible Web pages (see W3C guidelines for example [3]), e-content can and should be more than just this. Students have so far been willing to struggle to access content because they really enjoy the interactivity, though a higher standard should be achieved. The Task

Force is working with NLN developers to improve interactivity and accessibility, and to help find alternative solutions for interactive content.

- It is vital to provide alternative text for graphics and images so that students using screen-reading software can access the information. The <alt> text should provide a description of the function of the image and not just a description of the image.
- The use of the 'longdesc' command is appropriate if a large amount of detailed description is required, for example, where a graph is described. Graphics should not be avoided as they can benefit individuals with certain learning difficulties or cognitive disabilities, though, of course, they should enhance the learning experience by including adequate text descriptions.

14.3.3 Visually-impaired students

- Students must be able to customise their font and colour settings. Often, designers use a large bold font in the belief that this enhances accessibility. Yet this may not suit an individual who prefers a small font. Contrasting colours are frequently used, and while this may prove ideal for one individual it is often unsuitable for another.
- Cluttered, illogically labelled and unpredictable pages and materials may be confusing for an individual using a screen magnifier.

14.3.4 Dyslexia

A major problem with the communications areas of most VLEs is the lack of a spell-checker. One solution is to prepare the message in Word, use the integrated spell-checking facility, and then copy and paste this into the VLE discussion board or email facility. Another alternative would be to use voice-recognition software. This is difficult and expensive for blind students, since additional bridging software is necessary to interface between the screen-reading software and the voice-recognition software. If the student experiences difficulty reading the text, it may be useful to change the size of the text or perhaps use a text reader.

It should be noted that many of the students who have been involved in the project so far have a high level of IT competency encompassing the use of assistive technology. Coyne and Nielsen [5] report that an individual using a screen reader finds it six times more difficult to access the Web (let alone e-learning) than an another individual using no assistive technology, assuming that all individuals are competent in using the technologies concerned. In our study, the students needed in most cases little assistance in using the VLE. They did, however, need some support in accessing the NLN materials but these would generally be used in a classroom situation in any case, where support would normally be available. However, it is clear that using and accessing e-learning requires students to contribute a substantial amount of time and effort, which may impinge on their learning experience. Research is currently being carried out to assess the amount of time spent in accessing and using software, and to compare the length of time required to perform the same task by mouse users, and students using screen readers and keystrokes.

The Task Force is fortunate in that, to up to a point, they can choose which VLE they wish to use and they have a high degree of control over the content. It is recognised that for many e-tutors of students with particular needs this will not be the case.

14.4 Specialist tutoring skills

The experience of e-tutoring over the past year has provided the Task Force with additional expertise to take e-learning forward to distance learning operation. This is not something that should be undertaken lightly. There are enormous support requirements, for example, relating to technical issues and material development, tutorial and pastoral support.

It is this experience and expertise that will be used to help extend e-learning in the College and to train other staff members. This is currently being done on a pilot basis. Staff will be participating in a six-week introductory course in Blackboard. This will give them the necessary technical skills as well as providing some additional information about online tutoring in general. Training will include three hours of face-to-face teaching, three hours of online teaching and some supplementary reading materials. The content will be structured around the use of NLN materials in the classroom to enhance and support 'traditional' learning and teaching. It is vital to ensure that the e-tutor has sound support in all teaching circumstances.

14.5 Conclusion

Advances in e-support and learning agents are ongoing, ensuring continued change in e-tutoring over the coming years. It is important to bear this in mind when planning implementation and staff development. With the development and implementation of interoperability standards and the widening use of metatagging, it will be easier to facilitate, find and select content for individual students. This will be a significant advance towards individualised learning. The process will become increasingly automated so that the e-tutor need only specify learning objectives, with the content automatically selected to suit the student's learning style and accessibility needs. Learning agents in the form of avatars will be available to prompt and, up to a point, even interact with the students when they get into difficulties with the materials, perhaps by providing alternative activities to reinforce the learning objectives or by pointing out further reading. Although this will not diminish the role of the e-tutor, it will certainly change it. On-going staff training will become necessary. These technological developments will provide the opportunity to focus on individualised learning and on supporting the student. It is vital, though, that the learning environment and content developers follow the World Wide Web accessibility guidelines and interoperability standards. The result can only be of tremendous benefit to disabled students and will be a major move towards equal learning opportunities for all.

"For people without disabilities, technology makes things convenient; for people with disabilities, it makes things possible." [6]

14.6 References

[1]   JISC TechDis service: **www.techdis.ac.uk**

[2]   IMS Guidelines for Developing Accessible Learning Applications – Version 0.6 White Paper, available from: **www.imsproject.org/ accessibility/ accwpv0p6/ imsacc_wpv0p6.html**

[3]   W3C Web Accessibility Initiative: **www.w3.org/WAI/**

[4]   Luke, R. (2002), AccessAbility: Enabling Technology for LifeLong Learning Inclusion in an Electronic Classroom, Educational Technology and Society, 5 (1)

[5]   Coyne, K.P. and Nielsen, J. (2001), Beyond ALT Text: Making the Web Easy to use for

Users with Disabilities. Nielsen Norman Group

[6]   Treviranus, J. (2000), Expanding the Digital Media in More Human Directions. Presented at the Towards the Digital Media Institute. University of Toronto: Knowledge Media Design Institute Lecture Series.

Chapter 15

Computer Mediated Conferencing case study: a JOB project student

Margaret Dilloway, Bournville College of Further Education
Simon Ball and **Allan Sutherland,** TechDis

15.1 Introduction

CMC as a term includes all forms of organised interaction between people, using computers or networks as the medium of communication. Romiszowski described CMC thus:

> "The attractions of CMC for future educational systems are many. First of all, it is one more particularly versatile approach to the delivery of distance education… However, there are other characteristics of CMC that are of value even if the educational process is not… carried out a distance. For example, the 'asynchronous' nature of interpersonal communication in a computer network, where individuals read messages and then respond in their own time, taking as long as they need to think out their responses, holds promise in certain contexts as compared to more conventional approaches to group discussion." [1]

In her book 'Tele-learning in a Digital World', Collis outlines the attributes of a successful CMC project [2]. They can be summarised as follows:

- clear and careful planning related to learning intentions, communication procedures and timelines,
- agreement amongst participating teachers on a common learning goal for the CMC project,
- including accommodation for events that happen at different times in participating institutions, such as holidays and examinations,
- having agreement on the mechanics of communication among the students (e.g. where individual responses are appropriate and where group responses are required; will anonymous postings be allowed?),
- having contingency plans in response to things not proceeding as anticipated – for example, when responses are not forthcoming or are of an unsatisfactory nature,
- having mutual agreement amongst participants

about the extent of expected communication,
- creating discussion among the teachers involved as to how assessment will be conducted.

CMC can also be used to give students an opportunity to interact with an 'expert' on a particular subject. This can be particularly relevant in vocational courses, where, for example, someone working in a travel agency can provide students of tourism with a valuable insight into the working practices involved in the industry. This communication could be asynchronous, via e-mail or a discussion board, or even synchronous, through chat or video conferencing.

This chapter will describe how a further education college has developed the use of CMC to provide vocational guidance to students with a disability. The project will be briefly outlined and illustrated using the experiences of one particular participant.

15.2 Case study: the JOB project

The JOB Project at Bournville College was created in 1998 and aims to deliver pre-vocational guidance and training to adults who are disabled, a user of the mental health service or who felt themselves disadvantaged in returning to the labour market. The training was delivered by the use of CMC, which students accessed either from their own homes or from local access centres. Through the CMC medium, students were able to communicate with one another and with their tutor, and take part in structured online learning activities.

The primary aim of the JOB programme was to provide people with disabilities with 24-hour access to vocational guidance via CMC. It also aimed to provide online training in computer-mediated tutoring, guidance and counselling to trainers, and to research and deliver mentoring training to tutors and guidance workers. Although students on the JOB Project were presented with a considerable amount of information in text format (within a resource room or library) or presented by the tutor, the main learning method was through discussion and peer-tutor interaction. The Open College Network has accredited the JOB Project.

15.3 A JOB project participant: Anne

When she joined the project, Anne was a 43-year-old woman with restricted mobility due to arthritis. She had spent much of her life in care and had spent a period living rough as a teenager, consequently her sense of self-worth and self-confidence were exceptionally low. She experienced bouts of depression in addition to her physical symptoms.

In conjunction with improvements in her personal life, Anne was encouraged to pursue her education and was offered a place on the JOB Project. She was placed in a cohort of 12 students who had been unable to access traditional educational establishments because of their disabilities and living patterns. Most of them attended numerous hospital appointments, and some experienced concentration problems due to the effects of medication, both of which can make traditional learning schemes problematic.

Anne discovered that she possessed an intellectual ability she had previously never known existed and exhibited a natural empathy for the needs of other students. The course included training in computer usage as well as development exercises such as confidence building, assertiveness training, form completion and interview technique.

Anne passed her course and subsequently enrolled with the Virtual Tutor Programme, another Open College Network accredited scheme. This course teaches trainers how to adapt their teaching methods to a remote format. Drawing upon her personal experiences of remote learning, and her prior lack of success in the traditional education system, she passed this course with distinction.

Anne's next step was a course delivered via CMC on Mentor Preparatory Training, delivered to people wishing to act as mentors or counsellors. Drawing further on her personal experiences she

achieved highly again. Following this she was asked by Bournville College to work as a trainer on another Virtual Mentor Programme. She performed well, ensuring all of her students completed the programme and received accreditation. She was able to tutor from her own home using the CMC delivery medium, fitting that tutoring around her lifestyle needs to minimise any aggravation of her physical symptoms. The CMC method enabled her to deliver training whereas she may have suffered anxiety in a comparable traditional teaching situation.

Moving on from this role, Anne gained employment in a school, working as a learning mentor to students who were in danger of exclusion, providing guidance and counselling as well as offering the students routes to other sources of assistance.

15.4 Conclusions

Anne considers herself 'one of the lucky ones' and writes "I hope that such courses will go on being funded so that many others can benefit – the ones with no confidence, disabled people, those with no formal education and so on. 'Virtual' students tend to bond and help others along no matter what time of day or night it is, as the computer is there and you can work when it suits you. Remote learning is the future; so let's make it possible for more students to get the chance to achieve their goals".

After much wrangling with various sources of funding, Bournville College is now creating a Virtual College 'NetBourn' to deliver remote training to people in the most disadvantaged wards of the City of Birmingham and to learners within their own homes. It appears likely that Anne will be offered employment as a Virtual Tutor.

Anne is not the only student to be enabled by the delivery of course materials online. The opportunity to create many more 'lucky ones' is open to the wider learning and teaching sector at present. The JOB Project can provide the sector with a good example of how participation can be widened simply by including a new method of delivery, and how, once initiated, the scheme can be self-perpetuating with those who succeed returning to ensure others can follow them. The Government has recently introduced several initiatives to pursue the Widening Participation agenda. The aim is to widen participation in post-16 education to 50% of all school-leavers. It is evident from this case study that remote learning, and CMC in particular, can be a valuable tool in achieving that goal.

Anne's experiences indicate that CMC can be of benefit to many students with apparent learning difficulties – not least because of the opportunities it affords for asynchronous participation [1]. It is evident that these opportunities will be maximised when a CMC programme is planned and agreed in advance in the ways proposed by Collis [2]. The experience of Anne also highlights the way in which CMC can be a useful medium to assist those who have teaching skills but who may not be able to facilitate learning through more traditional media.

15.5 References

[1]   Romiszowski, A.J. (1997), Web-Based Distance Learning and Teaching, in: Badrul, H. Khan (Ed.) Web-Based Instruction, New Jersey: Educational Technology Publications.
[2]   Collis, B. (1996), Tele-learning in a Digital World. London: International Thomson Computer Press.

Editor's Note
Anne is a pseudonym given to the student in the case study described in this chapter by the editors in order to protect her right to anonymity.

Dyslexia-friendly computer-based learning materials

Chapter 16

Nigel Beacham, Loughborough University

16.1 Introduction

Until recently, ways in which students with learning difficulties can improve their learning by using computers have tended to be overlooked in education. This chapter focuses on the ways in which people who have dyslexia can improve their learning by using computers without inhibiting other types of learner. One solution has been to use multiple media. This approach to learning employs several senses with the intention of achieving improved comprehension of the information presented. There is a large body of research claiming employment of multiple media can improve the learning of all learners, including dyslexics. Furthermore, there is a growing consensus among researchers of educational technology that learning materials should be designed for all types of learners and learning styles (including people who have dyslexia), rather than being allowed to simply reflect the tutor's preferred style of teaching.

Despite the evidence in support of multiple media, it remains unclear how to effectively use combinations of media. When learning materials are produced, many subconscious assumptions are made about the types of media appropriate for the task and how they should be combined. It is also often assumed that what is good for one type of learner is good for all, including dyslexics. Two important factors that are often overlooked are the sub-modality properties of the media best suited for a task domain and individual differences in perception, coding and recall of verbal and nonverbal information.

With these factors in mind, this chapter provides an outline of some of the difficulties faced by dyslexic learners when learning using computer-based learning materials. Possible reasons for these difficulties are then explained based upon current dyslexia research. A general cognitive theory is used as a framework to explain how combinations of media can affect dyslexics during learning and how these combinations could be better used. The findings of a recent study are prsented examining this understanding of the learning experience of dyslexics and how combinations of media within computer-based learning materials can affect the experience.

16.2 Dyslexic difficulties

The author has used the following definition of dyslexia:

> "Dyslexia is one of several distinct learning disabilities. It is a specific language-based disorder of constitutional origin characterised by difficulties in single word decoding, usually reflecting insufficient phonological processing abilities. These difficulties in single-word decoding are often unexpected in relation to age or other cognitive abilities; they are not the result of generalised developmental disabilities or sensory impairment. Dyslexia is manifested by a variable difficulty with different forms of language, including, in addition to a problem with reading, a conspicuous problem with acquiring proficiency in writing and spelling."[1]

This definition is particularly appropriate because it is derived from a cognitive perspective. Because of their difficulties in single word decoding and their insufficient phonological processing abilities, dyslexics have weaknesses in many other cognitive abilities, not only those related to language-based tasks. These include:

- short-term memory limitations,
- difficulty processing sound,
- difficulty with co-ordination and motor skills,
- difficulty with visual processing.

As a result, dyslexics often have difficulty performing many of the following activities:

- reading and writing,
- organisation and time management,
- remembering and concentrating,
- learning and understanding,
- recognising and recalling,
- finding and navigating.

Although dyslexics can benefit from computer-based learning materials more than traditional teaching methods, they can still experience difficulties with the tasks listed above. Using computer-based learning materials, they are still likely to:

- re-read textual material,
- read slowly,
- misread words,
- lose their place,
- find it difficult to focus on the screen/page,
- find unfamiliar vocabulary difficult to learn,
- be distracted due to conditions such as pattern glare.

It is therefore necessary to consider multiple media approaches to teaching to help people with dyslexia. It is necessary to consider whether computer-based learning materials should be developed where information is represented in several appropriate sensory forms, or whether specific types of information should be targeted to specific senses depending upon the particular task requirements.

There are many studies about the effectiveness of multimedia and learning styles in educational systems, but very few give an insight into why some combinations of media are more effective than others when used by people with learning difficulties such as dyslexia. It is therefore unclear whether media combinations affect both dyslexic and non-dyslexic learners in the same way. Furthermore, experiments that have examined the effects of different media combinations on learning have been constructed over simple subject domains. One reason for this might be because over-complex subject domains require an extensive set of learning materials to ensure the majority of learners (including dyslexics) develop the necessary level of understanding. One dilemma is that often subjects at higher education level tend to lean towards complex subject domains. There seems to be no theoretical framework that is able to account for all of the factors at work in complex subject domains. One reason for this can be attributed to the way theories have developed separately within different disciplines.

In the same way as theories of cognition in reading and writing, so theories of dyslexia and multimedia have also been developed separately. There is a need for general theories that provide a framework for these separate theories, a framework that can explain how different media types affect the learning process of dyslexics and non-dyslexics and their relation to other types of learners with individual differences. Such a framework is important if computer-based learning materials are to be designed to effectively teach courses with such a varied and complex group of learners. Dual coding theory is one theory that provides a framework in which aspects of these given theories can be united.

16.3 Dual coding theory

According to Paivio's dual coding theory, information is processed through one of two generally independent channels [2]. One channel processes verbal information such as text and audio and the other channel processes visual information such as diagrams, animations and photographs. Paivio also suggests two different types of internal representational unit: 'imagens' for mental images and 'logogens' for verbal entities. Logogens are organized in terms of associations and hierarchies while imagens are organized in terms of part-whole relationships. Three types of internal processing are identified: representational – the direct activation of verbal or non-verbal representations; referential – the activation of the verbal system by the nonverbal system or vice-versa; and associated processing – the activation of related presentations within the same verbal or nonverbal system.

Studies by Paivio and others suggest that by choosing an appropriate combination of media, learning outcomes can be improved. For example, information that uses verbal and relevant visual illustrations together is likely to be learned better than information that uses text alone, audio alone, a combination of text and audio, or illustrations alone. An auditory medium can be better than textual information for remembering a small amount of verbal information for a short period. For retaining information over longer periods, text can be better than sound for communicating information. When the visual channel is already being used, it can be more appropriate to use audio verbal information than textual information. Objects are better recalled and recognised using nonverbal than verbal information. There are exceptions however, for example when items are conceptually similar or when items are presented so quickly that verbal labels cannot be created for nonverbal information. Nonverbal information is not as good at communicating abstract concepts as verbal communication. Nonverbal information is, however, good at communicating spatial information and helping to recognise and recall spatial relationships. McLoughlin supports the notion of dual processing being central to dyslexia. He provided three principles that are not only derived from a working memory model but also can be associated with dual coding theory [3].

▶ make it manageable: reduce the load on working memory and avoid dual processing wherever possible,

▶ make it multi-sensory: increase the power of the encoding by use of a variety of stimuli,

▶ make use of memory aids: to facilitate recall.

While these principles are helpful when applied to personal, learning and work settings, it is not entirely true that dual processing should be avoided in every situation.

It has been shown that dual coding can impair multimedia learning and that understanding is best achieved when learning stimuli match encoding stimuli. For example, when pictures accompany a short story they can interfere with a poor reader's ability to learn sight vocabulary. However, as presented in the next section, there are plenty of situations where dual processing can be used to reduce load on working memory and help improve learning. Therefore, it is important to investigate when dyslexics should and should not avoid dual processing when using multi-sensory approaches such as computer-based learning.

At present, with respect to computer-based learning, few multi-sensory approaches have been properly evaluated to show that they make a significant difference when compared to giving dyslexics more contact with a qualified support tutor. The next section aims to explain some of the possible differences in the representational systems between dyslexics and non-dyslexics, based on dual coding theory.

16.4 Dyslexic differences

This section outlines some of the main characteristics of dyslexia from the perspective of dual coding theory and explains how, using this theory, computer-based learning materials can be developed to help improve dyslexics' learning.

Characteristics of dyslexics include:

▶ finding concrete words easier to encode, recognise and recall than abstract words,

▶ taking longer than non-dyslexics to name very familiar objects,

▶ visualising text using graphical-motor skills rather than auditory-motor skills,

▶ not using auditory-motor skills effectively in order to prevent modality-specific visual overload,

▶ being distracted by imagery,

▶ having difficulties in retrieving verbal information from long-term memory,

▶ having difficulties with memory span for verbal information,

▶ being able to remember fewer verbal items,

▶ being able to hold fewer long words than short words in memory,

▶ having a limited sight vocabulary,

▶ having sound blending problems,

▶ having phonological representations either poorly specified or inaccessible,

▶ having difficulty recalling and pronouncing certain words,

▶ having problems establishing new phonological representations,

▶ showing poor reading of non-words,

▶ making more errors when repeating low frequency words than high frequency words,

▶ being able to read regular words faster than irregular words,

▶ tending to omit function words such as 'for' and 'the',

▶ tending to use visual skills to compensate for their phonological deficit,

▶ differing in their contrast sensitivity at low but not high spatial frequencies.

From these characteristics of dyslexics the following list of guidelines has been formed. The guidelines are intended to help content developers and dyslexics themselves develop 'dyslexia friendly' learning materials.

▶ communicate key points using where possible concrete words and language,

▶ where possible only use abstract words and language when sure learners have a good understanding of what the abstract word means,

▶ define abstract words and concepts using concrete words and pictures,

▶ use repetition of keywords to reinforce learning of important words,

▶ label familiar objects if they are central to the learning task,

▶ where possible encourage learners to use auditory-motor skills to learn textual information (i.e., to repeat what the textual information says in their heads and reflect what the information means to them),

- to remove visual information when being tested, if initial information only contained verbal information,
- give more time for encoding, recognising and recalling of verbal information from long-term memory,
- allow more time for coping strategies to be applied and compensating for phonological deficit,
- break information into smaller more manageable chunks (i.e. no more than 3-4 items as opposed to 7-9),
- where possible reduce the amount of previously presented information needed to be recalled if it is not central to the learning objectives,
- take account of the number of short and long words expected to be retained in memory at any one time and make sentences simple and concise where possible,
- only encourage learners to remember verbal words that are necessary,
- encourage the development of sight vocabulary through repetition, sounding words and providing referential and associative links to other verbal and nonverbal information (particularly related to prior knowledge),
- where possible use audio to give learners a phonological understanding of how non-words and symbols are referred,
- lower the contrast between background and fonts, and provide plenty of white space to reduce contrast sensitivity effects,
- where possible use regular words instead of irregular words,
- refrain from underlining text.

16.5 Research findings

The above guidelines were used in a recent study by the IMPACT Research Group, at the Department of Computer Science in Loughborough University, which investigated whether media combinations have an affect on dyslexics' learning and whether the effects are consistent with non-dyslexics.

The results from the study of media combinations offer the following preliminary findings:

- learning scores do differ between dyslexics and non-dyslexics for different media combinations,
- the different media combinations can improve dyslexics' understanding but not in the same way as for non-dyslexics,
- computer-based learning materials can be

pitched at the same level for both dyslexic and non-dyslexic learners and do not need to be extensive, but instead more focused towards the core subject,
- a dual coding theory approach helps measure and compare the amount of computer-based learning material learned by dyslexics and non-dyslexics,
- dyslexics' previous knowledge is allowed for by facilitating recognition and recall of items,
- dyslexics' different learning styles and strategies (including those used for coping) can be considered by making the materials available online after the initial learning session.

Other interesting results from the study show that dyslexic learners tend to score lower than non-dyslexics. This indicates that dyslexics are disadvantaged and only through extra work can they make up this learning deficit. The findings also indicate that novice learners who are dyslexic are more susceptible to incurring poor assessment scores because of a 'knock-on' effect when presented with materials that build on existing materials.

Consistent with dual coding theory, novice learners who are dyslexic are also more affected by the media combination than those dyslexics who are familiar with the materials. Interestingly, some dyslexics score better with text alone than with text and diagrams, and some dyslexics score better with text and diagrams than with text alone. Although it is uncertain why this occurs, there are also different sub-types of dyslexia that may be defined by different strengths (research in this field is ongoing) and this may account for these findings.

The evidence does seem to suggest that using concrete, high frequency, and familiar words can help dyslexic learners' comprehension. Furthermore, within certain situations, such as an electronic lecture, supplementing nonverbal information with verbal information in the form of audio can be better than textual information. It can reduce the amount of nonverbal processing necessary to understand the meaning of information.

16.6 Conclusions

This chapter has explained how dyslexic learners were helped to learn with computer-assisted learning materials designed using a dual coding theory approach. Particular attention has been paid to the human cognition and learning theory aspects of dyslexia in order that a better understanding is formed of how dyslexics are helped to learn using computers. As described in this chapter, much of the research conducted has focused on the indicators of dyslexia and the presentation and delivery of learning materials to help facilitate learning. Instead of a behavioural approach, this chapter advocates a cognitive approach called dual coding theory to explain the individual differences of learners who have dyslexia.

The following findings have been observed using dual coding theory as a framework for analysing the way dyslexic learners learn. It is important that a multi-sensory approach to learning takes account of the type of media combination used; that high frequency words are used whenever possible and low frequency words formally introduced; that low frequency words are first introduced using pictures and then are regularly used without pictures; that concrete nouns are used whenever possible as opposed to abstract nouns; that learning materials are well laid out and structured; that there exist opportunities to go over the learning material in various ways; that people who have dyslexia have an understanding of how verbal representations are formed whilst learning. Dual coding theory is a well-established general theory of human cognition that can be used to develop and evaluate computer-based learning materials regardless of individual differences.

16.7 References

[1]   Orton Dyslexia Society, (1994), A new definition of dyslexia, Bulletin of the Orton Dyslexic Society, Fall.

[2]   Paivio, A. (1971), Imagery and verbal processes, New York, Rinehart and Winston.

[3]   McLoughlin, D. (2001), Adult dyslexia: assessment, counselling and training. In Hunter-Carsch, M and Herrington, M (eds) Dyslexia and effective learning: in secondary and tertiary education, London, Whurr Publishers.

Chapter 17

The development of an institutional Web policy: a case study

Michael Lakey, Tynemouth College

17.1 Introduction

This short chapter has a dual purpose. First, it is written to explore Web accessibility policy development by outlining the personal aspect of the process; that is, the steps by which practitioners become aware of the need to address these issues. Second, it seeks to illustrate this process within an institutional context at Tynemouth College.

To these ends, this chapter has three sections. The first section explores the personal development underlying the experiences of Web and education professionals writing HTML materials with accessibility in mind. The second section outlines the process of institutional development by which a set of accessibility criteria were compiled. The final section of the chapter comprises of an example of the completed Web accessibility policy.

17.2 Personal development

It is appropriate to begin an examination of Web accessibility policy development at this **personal** level because, particularly in education, it is personal interest that has historically driven much ICT-based activity. Especially in smaller institutions, ICT specialists tend to inherit network management roles whilst non-ICT specialists often find themselves in the situation of being required to publish learning materials in a Web based format. Members of staff in this situation tend to have only a partial grasp of the appropriateness of electronic media and of the technical and pedagogical skills necessary to effectively develop educational solutions that translate the full range of classroom-based learning activities. Consequently, whilst ICT infrastructure in many institutions is adequate, the extent to which it is used as a learning medium greatly depends upon the experience of staff and upon their classroom requirements. Moreover, the central educational activity in many institutions remains classroom-

based, which means that usually ICT is at most a supporting player in learning. As a result, the focus of staff development in ICT skills is contingent upon the needs of particular students for whom staff produce materials. If, for instance, there are no students with sensory impairment in a particular cohort, then it is less likely that staff will perceive the need to develop skills in accessible publishing. This situation is addressed by the anticipatory clauses in the Special Educational Needs and Disability Act (2001). This process also reflects the experience of support staff.

The author of this case study originally developed an interest in Web development whilst working as a research assistant at a higher education institution. Nevertheless, as the post expanded to include the authoring of HTML-based materials on CD-ROM, accessibility issues became increasingly important. As the goal of the CD-ROM project was to publish the materials for as wide a student audience as possible, a number of technical and design questions arose:

17.2.1 Technological issues:
- what is the most appropriate format for CD-ROM/Web: Word, Flash, PDF or HTML?
- how do different proprietary browsers deal with text, images, frames and scripts?
- what differences exist between different versions of the same browser?
- what are the capabilities of non-visual browsers?
- what is the anticipated technological competence of the user?

17.2.2 Design issues:
- to what extent ought images to be used?
- what is the best mode of navigation through the site?
- how can a consistent house style be maintained whilst ensuring that those who need to adjust the on-screen display are able to do so?

Clearly, several of these items are concerned more with aesthetics and interoperability than with accessibility. Nevertheless, aesthetics, interoperability and accessibility are interrelated. As Microsoft and Netscape browsers use slightly different HTML, any attempt to ensure that the CD-ROM displayed equally well for all users necessarily involved some examination of issues of cross-browser compliance. A consistent approach to cross-browser compliancy led to a consideration of the requirements of additional standards, such as those used by non-visual browsers. Needless to say, in the early stages of the project the apparently important issues were those on which, historically, Microsoft and Netscape browsers have differed, such as, frames, margins and scripting for animations. Once these issues were resolved it was realised that compatibility issues of equal difficulty existed for users of non-visual browsers. How would these browsers render visual components of a page, such as an image, animation or a frame? Accessibility issues had become highly important.

17.3 Institutional development

Since November 2000, the author of this chapter worked as a Web Developer at Tynemouth College, North Shields. This college has a contract with Research Machines who provide network support and network infrastructure. In terms of hardware and software, the network is a series of Windows NT 4 servers and around 200 Windows 98 client workstations. Web publishing is FrontPage 98/2000 based with several server-side facilities, such as ODBC database management, administered on client machines via the FrontPage extensions. As the intranet and Internet sites were established projects, it was not feasible to redesign the sites entirely from scratch once the academic year had begun. Rather, a review of the sites was initiated, with a view to evaluating both their logical and technical structure. The review included accessibility issues.

One major cause for concern was the use of FrontPage 'navigation components' such as hover buttons. FrontPage 98 hover buttons are an easy way of producing navigation buttons with mouseover effects whilst avoiding the use of images. However, as they rely on Java Applets to work, they are liable to be a problem for non-visual browsers. Their output is not ordinarily accompanied by a text alternative, which means that those designers who wish to use them must either specify an alternative page or provide redundant text links. Second, the hyperlink is actually a parameter of the Java Applet, which means that it is not recognized by non-visual

browsers as a hyperlink in the conventional sense. This makes it unreadable. Third, as the buttons are not rendered as images or as text, they are not browser resizable, which means that users of Microsoft or Netscape browsers who need to resize page elements in order to read them are unable to do so. As much of the site depended upon this technology, much redesign work became necessary.

This redesign process had two major constraints. On one side, the focus upon accessibility, all the more necessary as it became evident that legislation was on its way, coupled with a preference for text above images and multimedia content tended towards a less 'animated', more controllable user experience. On the other side, the use of the Internet site as a marketing tool meant that an engaging and appropriate use of multimedia technologies was appropriate. Whilst the intranet site was, by virtue of its internal nature, less marketing oriented, the Internet site was produced in two versions: one in Flash and one in HTML to ensure accessibility. Both sites were launched in time for the following academic year.

This was facilitated by an institutional structure that in several respects lent itself to a coordinated accessibility strategy. Tynemouth College shares its Learning Resources Director with another further education college in the region. As a result of this, there were many informal links between the Learning Resources teams in both institutions and Web developers from both institutions discussed accessibility issues on a regular basis. Initially, this informal consultation was limited to specific issues, such as assessing proprietary accessibility products, such as Bobby [1]. However, in anticipation of the Special Educational Needs and Disability Act (2001), this relationship was formalized. A checklist of minimum standards of accessibility for all Web publications was compiled by the Web development team, which could be implemented at both institutions. After some research a draft policy was compiled that was loosely based upon the W3C accessibility checkpoints [2]. This draft policy (see Section 17.4) was sent for committee approval at each institution.

17.4 Case study: a draft accessibility policy for Web-based publications

The draft accessibility policy that was drawn up as a result of collaboration between learning resources and Web development staff in two institutions is presented verbatim here.

Preamble

"The power of the Web is in its universality. Access by everyone regardless of disability is an essential aspect."
(Tim Berners-Lee, W3C Director and inventor of the Web)

The College aims, as far as is reasonably possible, to ensure that any document, resource or page is accessible to all students regardless of any disability. To this end the College seeks to ensure that all Web-based publications comply with widely recognised standards in Web publishing. In particular, College publications will be encouraged to meet the standards laid out in the W3C guidelines for Web Accessibility.

Policy

These standards are categorised into priorities depending upon the importance to a disabled user. The college aims to fully implement all W3C Priority 1 criteria and wherever feasible, W3C Priority 2 criteria under these guidelines. These Priorities are defined as follows:

Priority 1: "A Web content developer must satisfy this checkpoint. Otherwise, one or more groups will find it impossible to access information in the document. Satisfying this checkpoint is a basic requirement for some groups to be able to use Web documents." [3]

Priority 2: "A Web content developer should satisfy this checkpoint. Otherwise, one or more groups will find it difficult to access information in the document. Satisfying this checkpoint will remove significant barriers to accessing Web documents." [3]

These priorities imply the use of a preferred format for Web delivery. This format is the HTML file written according to W3C's HTML 4.0 specifications. As such, any documents in other formats should be solely available for printing purposes and published alongside HTML pages that serve as online versions of the printable information.

Checklist

The following list of guidelines relate to Priority 1 concerns and are therefore mandatory for all who wish to publish to College servers:

▶ provide a text equivalent for every non-text

element,
▶ ensure that all information conveyed with colour is also available without colour,
▶ clearly identify changes in the natural language of a document's text and any text equivalents,
▶ organize documents so they may be read without style sheets,
▶ ensure that equivalents for dynamic content are updated as the page changes,
▶ avoid causing the screen to flicker,
▶ use the clearest and simplest language appropriate for a site's content,
▶ provide redundant text links for each active region of a server-side image map,
▶ where possible client-side image maps instead of server-side image maps,
▶ for data tables, identify row and column headers,
▶ for data tables that have two or more logical levels of row or column headers, use markup to associate data cells and header cells,
▶ title each frame to facilitate frame identification and navigation,
▶ ensure that pages are usable when all programmatic objects are turned off or not supported,
▶ provide an auditory description of the important information any visual track in multimedia presentations,
▶ for any time-based multimedia presentation synchronise equivalent alternatives (e.g., captions or auditory descriptions of the visual track) with the presentation,
▶ if, after best efforts, you cannot create an accessible page, provide a link to an alternative page that is accessible.

The following issues relate to Priority 2 criteria. As such, they are not mandatory, but do embody good practice. All staff are expected to work towards complying with the items on this list:

▶ ensure that foreground and background colour combinations contrast,
▶ use style sheets to control layout and presentation,
▶ use relative rather than absolute units in page design,
▶ do not cause other windows to appear without informing the user,
▶ divide large blocks of information into manageable groups,
▶ identify the target of each hyperlink,
▶ use consistent navigation mechanisms,

17.5 Conclusions

The case study of an institutional Web accessibility policy presented in this chapter is the result of two important factors: personal experience and commitment to accessibility issues and collaboration between staff from different departments and institutions. The policy is based on an internationally known and accepted set of accessibility standards [3]. A policy on its own will not change practice, but if it launched well within a institution it can set the tone in which further developments will follow.

17.6 References

[1] **www.cast.org**
[2] **www.w3.org/TR/1999/
WAI-WEBCONTENT-19990505/
full-checklist**
[3] Chisholm, W., Vanderheiden, G. and Jacobs,
I. (1999), Web Content Accessibility
Guidelines 1.0 W3C Recommendation,
available from:
**www.w3.org/TR/1999/
WAI-WEBCONTENT-19990505**

5

Implications for personal and professional practice

Chapter 18

So what does all this mean for me?

Jane Seale, University of Southampton and Kings College, London

18.1 Introduction

The purpose of this whole book has been to outline and describe how technologies can be used to meet the needs of disabled students. It has focused on two important issues. Firstly, how assistive technology can facilitate access to learning resources and teaching material. Secondly, how e-learning materials and learning technologies that utilise the Web need to be carefully designed so that all students can benefit from using them. This chapter will attempt to provide a concluding overview of all the chapters within this book by drawing out the main themes and issues and placing them within the context and experience of individual staff that work in further and higher education.

18.2 Who is responsible?

18.2.1 Personal responsibilities
Staff within further and higher education are having to respond to a number of externally driven initiatives, and there must be occasions when some, if not all of us, despair at what we perceive to be extra responsibilities that are loaded upon us.

The Special Educational Needs and Disability Act (2001) and its legal implications clearly indicate that responsibility has to be taken for ensuring accessible and inclusive learning environments within further and higher education. It may be tempting for individuals to assume that their institution will bear all the responsibility. However, as Willder outlined in Chapter 2, a number of professionals within an institution will have to change their practice:

- lecturers will need to be prepared to assist, for example by providing lecture notes in alternative formats,
- those involved in marketing an institution will need to assist, for example by providing accessible prospectuses,
- admissions staff will need to assist, for example by ensuring that application forms are usable and accessible and creating systems whereby disabled students feel comfortable disclosing their needs,
- library staff will need to assist, for example by working to ensure that online information services are accessible,
- IT staff will need to assist, for example by anticipating student needs and planning how to meet those needs.

We will all differ on whether we see these responsibilities as an exciting challenge or a wearisome burden. What may influence our view is the extent to which we feel we are supported by our departments and institutions. If departments and institutions take their responsibilities seriously then individuals should not feel overwhelmed by these new responsibilities.

18.2.2 Departmental responsibilities
In Chapter 12 Peacock, Ross and Skelton presented a case study of how Queen Margaret University College had begun to work towards improving staff awareness of accessibility legislation. This work involved the whole of the institution including a network of departmental special needs co-ordinators. The role of a departmental special needs co-ordinator may vary, but in general they act as a liaison between the student and the departmental staff. They communicate with students about their needs, and then pass this information on to all those staff

that may need to respond to these needs in some way. Co-ordinators are useful because it means that students do not suffer the embarrassment or inconvenience of having to contact each individual member of staff and repeat over and over again what they require. This can be very important for those students who are anxious not to draw attention to themselves.

Co-ordinators cannot work in isolation, however, and it is vital that their departments, through managers and teaching committees, create an environment and culture in which the co-ordinator will be 'heard' and responded to. It is also important that the role and responsibilities of the co-ordinator are clearly defined and that the existence of such a role is not interpreted by other departmental staff as a reason not to get involved.

Hall and Tinklin presented some case studies of the experiences of disabled students in Scottish higher education [1]. In discussing what factors influenced the positive experiences of students, they highlighted the fact that for some students departmental contacts were influential – when they were knowledgeable and committed. However they also warn that not all students could be guaranteed good treatment from their departmental contacts.

> "Some disability contacts volunteered to take on the role, others were just told they would do it. This tends to affect their level of commitment to the job"

18.2.3 Institutional responsibilities

Throughout this book we have heard how important it is for an institution as a whole to respond to the new responsibilities that the Special Educational Needs and Disability Act (2001) will bring. We have also heard that a number of factors will influence institutions attempts to respond to the Act. For example, in Chapter 17 Smith described how individual commitment and group collaboration influenced the development of a Web accessibility policy at his institution. While in Chapter 9 Witt and McDermott noted that although some institutions may attempt to adopt a corporate approach to Web accessibility (where there is a co-ordinated approach, central support, tight content management and strict design standards) this may meet with some resistance for departments who have created their own style, design and content. In Chapter 11 Cann, Ball and Sutherland argued that institutions who have already purchased or are thinking of purchasing a Virtual Learning

Environment will need to have an open dialogue with vendors in order to ensure that equal accessibility for all users is a high priority. The high proportion of vendors not having a publicly available accessibility policy statement in the study by Cann, Ball and Sutherland, is perhaps a little alarming.

In Chapter 12, Peacock, Ross and Skelton presented a case study of how Queen Margaret University College had begun to work towards improving staff awareness of accessibility legislation. They stated that two groups had been fundamental to the success of the development and evaluation of a staff development module. The first of these was QMUC's Roundtable: a cross-institutional group consisting of librarians, academic staff, technology professionals, students and administrative staff. This Roundtable has worked to develop recommendations to enhance teaching and learning through the use of technology and to improve communication and collaboration amongst its members and across the institution. The importance of initiatives like the Roundtable approach is they can help to prevent new initiatives being seen as enforced from the top down and can help to place these initiatives within an organisation context.

The Roundtable methodology employed by QMUC has been developed by Gilbert and Ehrmann of the AAHE TLT Group in the US. In reflecting on the use of this methodology to promote the use of learning technologies within their institutions, Oliver and Kemp stated:

> "Gilberts' notion of a Roundtable implies a gathering together of disparate institutional elements to focus on a collective purpose. This reflects the Roundtable of Arthur and his knights where a vision – the Holy Grail Quest – had to be created and then made to happen. The knights/members had to buy in to resolve and then realise it, often away from the Roundtable itself. In many ways our Holy Grail is both as illusory and as potent as theirs and like theirs may also be fully realised only in later assessments and re-workings long after the Roundtables themselves have ceased to exist or have become something else. Ultimately for us what will be measured is the impact on hearts and minds and on learning." [2]

It strikes me that in all institutions, irrespective of whether or not they employ a Roundtable approach, there will need to be an element of 'buying in' to the principles of accessibility and inclusivity. However, the Special Educational Needs and Disability Act (2001) means that the goals of accessibility and inclusivity cannot be 'illusory', and legislation on its own cannot change hearts and minds. Institutions will need to work hard to make the goals of accessibility and inclusivity very concrete and real. As Dilloway, Ball and Sutherland indicate in Chapter 15, this will involve a great deal of planning and forward thinking. It may also require some highly visible 'champions' for the cause.

18.3 Staff development

A number of chapters in this book have stressed the importance of staff development. For example, Willder argued in Chapter 2 that satisfactory implementation of the legislation and avoidance of liability will require staff training and raising of awareness. Institutions may approach staff development in different ways. They may develop training materials similar to the WebCT module developed and described by Peacock, Ross and Skelton in Chapter 12. Alternatively they may choose to run workshops or distribute guidelines. Staff development departments may also play an important role as an 'information broker', pointing academic staff to the wealth of information that is available from organisations such as TechDis and RNIB.

Staff development activities such as workshops are often one-off events aimed at individuals, and those responsible for staff development may find it more profitable to work with whole departments in more interactive and longer lasting activities. There may also be scope for identifying potential 'champions' of accessibility and inclusivity and offering them a tailored portfolio of training opportunities with a view to encouraging them to cascade and disseminate their knowledge to others within their areas or departments.

A number of institutions have developed new lecturers programmes, which are often accredited by the Institute for Learning and Teaching. Within these programmes new lecturers are introduced to principles and theories underlying good teaching and learning. Such programmes offer a good opportunity for influencing new hearts and minds and it would appear important that the principles of accessibility and inclusivity are included within the curricula of such programmes.

Whilst training is an important issue to consider

when thinking about how to change practice and implement new accessibility and inclusivity initiatives, it is imperative that institutions and those responsible for staff development also consider support issues. Ensuring accessibility and inclusivity will require an on-going commitment from staff and this in turn will mean that they will require on-going support. For example, Evans in Chapter 14 argues that it is vital to ensure that those responsible for e-tutoring disabled students have sound support in all teaching circumstances.

18.4 Technology on its own is not a panacea

One of the overriding messages from this book is that the potential that technologies hold to improve the accessibility and inclusivity of tertiary education for disabled students will be highly influenced by the staff that design, develop, use and support them. For example, in Chapter 4, Neumann argues that technology will fail to deliver results if we accept 'poor and narrow-minded design'. In Chapter 8, Sloan warns of the dangers of assuming that specialised technological tools will absolve us from all responsibility:

> "Even with an authoring tool specifically designed to create fully accessible content, it is vital for content authors to be aware of accessible design techniques, particularly in light of the current constraints affecting Web development environments".

Henderson, in Chapter 7 also gives us an important reminder that high-tech tools do not necessarily ease the burden for students. He argues:

> "The greater the complexity of the solution, the more we ask of the user."

The sentiment of the arguments of Neumann, Sloan and Henderson is that technology on its own, no matter how new and innovative cannot effect change or 'produce' accessible and inclusive learning resources. Good practice will rely on a partnership between staff, students, departments and institutions in order to avoid the trap that Wiles warns of in Chapter 13:

> "We must not fall into the trap of allowing innovation in technology to outstrip its usefulness as a tool that enables accessibility…"

18.5 Matching appropriate technology to student needs

One of the main messages of this book has been about the need for individuals and institutions to start addressing the needs of disabled students. One important principle underlying this message is that of not assuming that all students who have a disability will have the same needs that can be met with the same technology. For example Wald in Chapter 5 notes that while institutions can do a great deal to ensure their policies and practice help to remove barriers to learning and participation, only the individual student can decide whether any particular technology is appropriate to meet their particular individual needs. While Draffan argues that all assistive technology has to be well matched to the user as there is such a wide choice available, it is important to understand the difficulties that each individual encounters in a teaching and learning situation. In Chapter 5, Wald concludes that it is important for student and institution to discuss these needs and how they can best be met.

These statements do not only apply to the formal assessment process that students might engage in with disability advisors or funding agencies, but also applies to the process that departments will need to engage in when deciding how they can support students who enter their programmes. The danger is that students will be assessed or assumed to need a particular technology or access solution because it is what is the institution has available. In the rehabilitation and special education field this would be called a 'supermarket' approach to assessment [3]. An alternative assessment model in this field has been proposed by Scherer and is called the 'matching persons to technology' model. This model was specifically designed to apply to high-tech assistive technologies, but the underlying principles could be applied to accessible and inclusive e-learning materials [4]. Scherer argues that when attempting to match technology to a person's needs the following things need to be considered:

▶ user (in our case student) goals and preferences,
▶ user's views of the benefits to be gained from a particular technology,
▶ changes in self-perceived functioning and outcome achievement over time.

One of the implications of this model is that student' needs and perceptions of the value of technologies may change over time, thus requiring a flexible approach to assessing and reviewing their needs. This will be a real challenge for institutions, who, in their response to the new legislation, may put systems and procedures in place that work against such flexibility.

18.6 Conclusion

The purpose of this chapter has been to highlight the main themes of the book and to place them with the context and experience of individual staff that work in further and higher education. This chapter has argued that while individuals cannot escape the responsibilities placed on them by the new SENDA legislation they can expect to be supported by their institutions. Institutions will need to support their staff by developing and agreeing institution-wide policies and guidelines as well as providing appropriate and timely staff development opportunities.

In attempting to address their new responsibilities, further and higher education staff will need to be aware that technologies on their own do not solve accessibility and inclusivity issues and that technology needs to be carefully and appropriate matched to the needs of disabled students. If staff take on board their responsibilities and increase their awareness and understanding of the issues then they are in a powerful position to really influence the teaching and learning opportunities of disabled students: responsibility + understanding = power. Or, in the words of Opitz:

> "The power of accessibility lies within the hands of the individuals, just as the power of the Internet lies within the empowerment of the individual". [5]

TechDis is working with organisations including the Association for Learning Technology, the Institute for Learning and Teaching, the Learning and Teaching Support Network and all funding councils to put the issues of technology and disabilities onto national agendas and ensure that staff are supported in their roles. TechDis is also looking at the technologies of the future and flagging potential issues for disabled students, both as barriers to learning and as new ways to access learning.

[1]   Hall, J. and Tinklin, T. (1998), Students First: The Experiences of Disabled Students in Higher Education. SCRE Research Report No 85. Available from: **www.scre.ac.uk/resreport/rr85/ index.html**

[2]   Oliver, M. and Kemp, C. (2001), Roundtables: realising the myth? Association for Learning Technology Newsletter, 34,4.

[3]   Nisbett, P and Poon, P (1998) Special Access Technology, Edinburgh, CALL Centre.

[4]   Scherer, M. and Craddock, G. (2001), Applying the Matching Person and Technology Evaluation Process, Library Hi Tech News, 18(1), 40-42.

[5]   Opitz, C. (2002), Online Course Accessibility: A Call for Responsibility and Necessity, Educational Technology Review, 10,(1). Available from: **www.aace.org/pubs/etr/optiz-xl.cfm**

© JISC TechDis Service and ALT